CHIEF

Leadership Lessons from a Village in Africa

Paul Seger

CHIEF

Leadership Lessons from a Village in Africa

Scripture quotations are from The Holy Bible, English Standard Version, copyright 2001 by Crossway, a publishing ministry of Good News Publishers. Used by permission. All rights reserved.

The cover photograph was taken by the author's father, Lionel Seger, who was a career missionary in Nigeria. The photo is of a typical Nigerian village in the 1960s with the tribal chief in the foreground. Many of the photographs in the book were also taken by Lionel Seger.

Cover by Ryan Seger and Lionstar Films

ISBN-13: 978-1483909332
ISBN-10:1483909336

CONTENTS

Preface...v

Acknowledgments ix

Introduction...xi

1. Village Chief or Medicine Man? 1
2. King of the Jungle...13
3. Lorries 25
4. Mai Haji 37
5. Anthills 47
6. Dodo...57
7. The First Rain..65
8. Hornbills...77
9. Mud Huts..91
10. The Blacksmith..103
11. Sawubona 119
12. Pushing Boulders...129
13. Veld Fires 143
14. Village Life 155
15. The Baobab Tree..165
16. Rhino Skin..175
17. Head Loads...183
18. Wells..191
19. The Swinging Bridge 199
20. Going Rogue...211

Appendix A 220

Appendix B 246

Appendix C 249

Notes 251

PREFACE

It was a remote village in northeastern Nigeria called Gadaka. My missionary parents positioned themselves in this village unaffected by the West. They were the first white people many had ever seen. It was remote. It was primitive. But it was home. This is where I grew up.

My dad had surveyed the area by air and knew there were many villages in this backcountry, so he drove in that direction. When he got to the end of the road, he just kept going until he got to Gadaka.

Dad built the first road into the area, and our Jeep pickup was the first motor vehicle in the region. It was so unique that men would work all day long for him breaking rock and loading the truck, just for the opportunity to ride. To them, it was as exciting as any Disney World attraction.

I learned Hausa, their national language, before I could speak English. I absorbed their culture before knowing much about my American heritage. Life was good. What a great place to grow up!

Daily, this little remote village demonstrated major leadership principles, but I didn't really learn them while I was there. It took some hindsight and experience in leadership to realize that those principles were there all the time. Amazingly, many of the simplest and most basic principles of leadership were found in a remote village in Africa.

The complexity of our Western world blurs our understanding of leadership. Thousands of books have been written on the topic. There are multiple theories of leadership, and each one seeks to replace the previous popular approach. So why would anyone write another book on leadership?

This is an attempt to simplify the topic. Looking at that remote setting of a village in Africa makes it possible to silence the noise of Western life and hear the drumbeat of basic leadership. Simple examples and illustrations from that village open windows to observe leadership in its most basic forms.

Leadership is simple and complex at the same time. It is simple—but not easy. This paradox complicates the topic.

The place to start is with the simple. Once that is mastered, it is possible to move into the complexity of leadership. This is a primer on the topic of leadership.

While the illustrations flow from my village, the principles originate in the Bible. Many books on the subject of leadership come from secular theorists. They would not claim to base their ideas in Scripture. Some would be violently opposed to anything Christian. Others plaster secular leadership models with Bible verses in an attempt to give them a Christian look. This book seeks to reflect the Bible with no apologies for doing so.

Truth originates with God. Sometimes non-religious people stumble onto principles that work. It didn't happen because they were searching Scripture. They just found something that seemed to function well. In many non-Christian leadership books there are practical hints that work. This book, however, is an attempt to bring to the surface biblical truths on the topic of leadership.

The Bible is not a textbook on the subject per se. No one book of the Bible is dedicated to teaching leaders how to lead. But embedded in the stories are rich illustrations of how to lead and how not to lead. The didactic sections give the principles by which a Christian should live and lead. It is assumed that any good and godly leader will possess these character traits.

Therefore, the premise for this book is that Scripture trumps any ideas on leadership we stumble upon. The Bible is the foundation for life and living. Even though I begin each chapter with an illustration from Africa, the Bible is the foundation and starting point of establishing truth.

ACKNOWLEDGMENTS

The Bible—the ultimate book on the subject of leadership. Thanks to God for His revelation of truth.

Thanks to all those who have impacted my life and influenced my philosophy of leadership. They are too numerous to list. A special thanks to Rick Oglesby and Paul Holritz for reviewing and improving the content of this book.

Ultimately, the most important impact on my life is my best friend and wife, Joan.

INTRODUCTION

Some people collect stamps. I collect definitions of leadership. There are hundreds to choose from. The definition we created for the organization I lead is: *A leader is a godly servant who knows where he is going and inspires and equips others to follow.* This one obviously has application to a Christian organization. Let's look at the key words.

GODLY - It is certainly possible to lead others and not be godly, but this is a definition for a Christian organization or church. The starting point is godliness. The traits of a leader in I Timothy 3 focus only on character. According to Scripture, character is more important than skills, knowledge, or personality. Imagine what it would be like to have a boss who always acted like Jesus. Leadership begins not with position—but with character.

SERVANT - Secular leadership models swing back and forth but ultimately come back to the idea of "servant leadership." This model happens to be the flavor of the day. But long before anyone wrote on the topic, Jesus was modeling leadership by washing the disciples' feet. Godly leadership constantly asks, "What can I do for you?"

KNOWS - A leader has confidence in his direction. It could be the wrong direction in spite of his conviction and enthusiasm. But he knows where he wants to go. That is one of the traits that attracts followers. People want to follow a person committed to forward movement.

GOING - Leadership is all about getting somewhere. Without leadership, a group of people are just standing around. Intrinsic to the idea of leadership is the idea that we are "here" and we want to get "there."

INSPIRES - Dictators drive people to compliance—but that is corrupt leadership. True leadership captures the hearts and emotions of others and tugs them forward with an irresistible force. Antoine de Saint-Exupery said, "If you want to build a ship, don't drum up people to collect wood and don't assign them tasks and work, but rather teach them to long for the endless immensity of the sea."[1]

EQUIPS - Good leaders provide the tools and training for others to move forward and to succeed. Leaders must be committed to helping others improve. The proof of good leadership is that the next generation goes further and faster. That happens through coaching and mentoring. The final report card of the effectiveness of a leader comes after he is gone.

FOLLOW - Intrinsic to any definition of leadership is the idea that someone is following. The common saying is that if you look around and no one is following, you are just out taking a walk. It is possible to have the corner office, but you are not a leader if no one is following.

This is the definition assumed in this book. Here it is again: *A leader is a godly servant who knows where he is going and inspires and equips others to follow.*

Leaders are both male and female. For ease of reference, I will take the liberty of simply using the male gender throughout this book.

1

VILLAGE CHIEF OR MEDICINE MAN?

Leading Without Title

Please, Lord, how can I save Israel?
Behold, my clan is the weakest in Manasseh,
and I am the least in my father's house.
Judges 6:15

A large chair does not make a king.
Sudanese proverb

L ike every other village in northeastern Nigeria, the town of Gadaka had a chief. He was the one who granted permission for Mom and Dad to live there. He gave them the land on which to build a house. He was in charge. Nothing of any consequence went on in that village unless he gave the okay.

When we wandered close to his hut, it was obligatory to stop and greet the chief. In contrast to the round huts of the rest of the villagers, his house was rectangular and slightly larger. The distinguishing characteristic of his "palace" was the thatch-covered front porch where groups of people always seemed to congregate. Some were his cadre of servants. Others were there seeking favors. Some just hanging out. Whatever official business took place in town happened at the chief's place and with his permission.

A village chief was a benevolent dictator. He was born into the position. Generation after generation handed down the autocratic mantle to their sons. It was a privileged position. The chief was supposed to have final authority. The villagers accepted his role, paid him homage, and submitted to his decisions.

In that remote village, away from civilization, there was structure. There was order. There was leadership.

But, this was not the only leadership in town. The chief was actually not the ultimate authority. Every village had another key player in the social structure: the medicine man. He was more witchdoctor than a medical doctor. He did not have a consulting room, but he accepted "patients" under the tree in front of his hut. His equipment was a bag full of feathers, herbs, bones, and a few dried vermin.

He did provide a version of healthcare for the village, however. A common prescription for ailments was bloodletting. This two-thousand-year-old remedy had found its way to the back regions of Africa. The tools of the trade were a homemade knife and a hollowed-out cow horn with a hole at the point. After slashing the skin, the practitioner would apply the horn and suck on the point, thus creating a vacuum that hastened the bleeding process.

His services, however, were for more than just physical problems. Villagers would seek his services to cast a spell on an enemy or to get a spell lifted. Whether you had a headache or an enemy, the medicine man was the key player in town. The reality was that the medicine man had more influence than the chief.

Animism was the predominant worldview in this village. The people believed there was deity in everything. They "saw" gods in lightning, trees, animals, mountains, and rocks. Their greatest fear was angry demons that needed to be appeased, and only the witchdoctor could fix that. This was beyond the power of the chief.

Even though the chief was the recognized leader, it was the medicine man that had the most influence. The chief had the title, but when it came to the most important issues of life, people followed the witchdoctor. The chief had position. The witchdoctor had power.

Kenneth Blanchard puts it this way: "The key to successful leadership today is influence, not authority."[2] One of the most fundamental principles of leadership is that a title does not make you a leader. The nameplate on the office door identifies a role in the organization. It does provide a platform. It can make it possible to command and control, but it doesn't make the resident of that room a leader.

Dictatorship is the lowest form of leadership. It could be argued that command and control is actually an absence of leadership. If you must force others, you are driving them, not leading. Like the village chief, the person in charge can demand compliance, but that is the antithesis of leadership.

Remember this book's proposed definition of leadership: *A leader is a godly servant who knows where he is going and inspires and equips others to follow.* Notice that nothing is said about position. Location on the organizational chart does not make a person a leader. Sometimes a title is conferred and the leader leverages that position. He may rise to the occasion to lead if a crown is placed on his head, but the true power of a leader is not in his position. This has always been the case. It was true in the village of Gadaka, Nigeria. The people had never read a book on leadership, but they illustrated this principle every day.

Mahatma Ghandi was a simple man without portfolio who changed a nation. His non-violent civil disobedience brought about independence for a nation and civil rights for people in South Africa and India. Without title or position, he campaigned for women's rights. He eased poverty. He led protests against the British-imposed salt tax. He was often imprisoned, but even that could not shut down his ability to lead. In fact, it accelerated it. Ghandi understood he could lead without position.

An intriguing meeting took place between two leaders—President Clinton and Mother Teresa. She was invited to speak at the 1993 National Prayer Breakfast in Washington, D.C. The President and Vice President were seated on the front row as this diminutive lady from India with no title or position began to speak.

She talked about Jesus and John the Baptist and how John leapt in the womb at the meeting of their mothers. The argument was that human life begins before birth. She went on to declare: "I feel that the greatest destroyer of peace today is abortion, because Jesus said, 'If you receive a little child, you receive me.' So every abortion is the denial of receiving Jesus."

There was an awkward silence in the ballroom that erupted into a standing ovation lasting several minutes. President Clinton and Vice President Gore remained seated. It was obvious who was leading in that room. She went on to say that abortion was "really a war against the child, and I hate the killing of the innocent child, murder by the mother herself. And if we accept that the mother can kill even her

5

own child, how can we tell other people not to kill one another? This is why the greatest destroyer of love and peace is abortion."[3]

The most powerful man in the world sat defenseless. Someone else was in charge at that moment. Mother Teresa was leading without title. Three thousand in the room followed her instead of the man with the title of President of the United States of America.

This principle is illustrated repeatedly throughout Scripture. Here are just a few of them.

For seven long years, the Midianites had ravaged the land of Israel. They would swarm in on camels, rape and pillage, and leave. The Jewish nation could not defend itself because it was severely outnumbered. In fear the citizens cowered in caves, dens, and strongholds.

Gideon was a not a person of significance. He was from the weakest clan and the youngest son of a most insignificant family in Israel, yet God picked him to be the liberator of Israel from the occupiers.

Those with title and authority did nothing to relieve the nation of the terrorists in the country, but Gideon reluctantly stepped forward. No one gave him a title. He didn't have a military commission or status. There was no reason why he, of all people, should lead the armies of Israel—but he did. He became one of the twelve judges of Israel. We have more verses and information about Gideon than of any other judge. We are still talking about him thousands of years later.

The story of David and Goliath is a classic illustration of this principle. When David showed up at the battle front, his brothers disdained this insignificant shepherd boy and told him to get back to his sheep. They chided him for daring to lead. Perhaps it was out of embarrassment. As soldiers with position they cowered at the threats of the giant. If anyone should have led the charge against Goliath, it should have been these well-armed and well-trained professionals. Yet David stepped forward as the least credentialed person on the battlefield. He led when others fled. Thousands of years later we are still talking about David because he refused to let the absence of a title keep him from leading.

Nehemiah also proved that one does not need a position to lead. He was dispensable. His job was to taste-test the food and wine for a king, so poison intended for the king would kill him instead. He could not go lower on the food chain—no one really cared if he died—yet he was the one who led the cause of rebuilding the walls of Jerusalem. It was his burden, vision, and passion that catapulted him into leadership.

The twelve disciples of Jesus were the most unlikely group of men ever to be leaders of the largest initiative ever launched on planet earth. This motley group of men held no official position in Israel. They were uneducated and rough around the edges. One was an anarchist and political activist.

Another was considered a traitor to his country as he collected taxes for a foreign occupier. Several were fishermen. None of them had a title. Yet God used them to initiate a movement that has now lasted 2000 years.

The Apostle Paul also demonstrated this principle on his boat ride to Rome. It is almost humorous. Paul was dragged before a court with irrational accusations as his enemies sought to get rid of him. It was either an act of desperation or a smooth move when he used his citizenship to his own advantage and appealed to Caesar. That earned him a free trip to Rome, but it was no Mediterranean cruise. He was a prisoner in chains. There was no one on that boat lower in the organizational chart than Paul. Yet, when Paul spoke, people listened. They acted. Repeatedly, Paul called the shots—and even the Captain acquiesced. Paul proved that leadership does not require a position.

The penultimate example of leadership without position was Jesus. He of course had position. He was God. But few in His day understood that and He held no title. He was born in poverty to unknown and insignificant parents. His name did not show up on the official political and religious leadership organizational charts. He grew up in the backwater village of Nazareth. Worked as a laborer. Lacked academic qualifications. No title. No portfolio. But no one could contest His ability to lead. It drove the establishment crazy. They couldn't process the idea that someone outside their structures could gather so many followers.

He was so effective that they eventually plotted his death. The Apostle John reports: *So the chief priests made plans to put Lazarus to death as well, because on account of him many of the Jews were going away and believing in Jesus* (John 12:10-11). The religious leaders were jealous of His success. It is amazing that spiritual leaders would think this way. It would be expected that common criminals and hit men would plot assassinations. But certainly this is not the demeanor of religious folk.

We could never imagine deacons and elders plotting the death of their pastor. These were the men who were supposed to lead the nation toward God. Here was the problem: they were watching their empire being eroded by an outsider with no portfolio. Obviously, Jesus was an incredibly effective leader.

All these stories illustrate the premise of this chapter: *you do not need a position or title to lead.* Head back to the village of Gadaka in northeastern Nigeria. Who was the true leader of that town? The "name-plate" on the chief's hut said one thing, but the villagers still headed down the path to the medicine man for the really important decisions in life.

Understanding this concept leads us to a couple of key principles.

If you have the title, don't assume you are the leader. It is a pitiful sight to watch a henpecked husband insist that he is the leader. It is sad to watch a young, inexperienced "leader" demand authority. It is even worse to live under the heavy hand of an autocratic dictator. Don't assume that your position on an organizational chart means anything. The person who just received the promotion may have the organizational clout, but that is totally different from being a leader.

If you are without a title, don't assume that you can't lead. Forget about position; rather seek to impact others. Don't seek advancement; rather find ways to serve others. Someone else may get the next job promotion, but that does not limit your leadership potential. The politics of your organization or business may be controlled by the powerbrokers, but ultimately, you don't need to be an insider to exercise leadership.

This principle shows up often in the church world. The assumed leader of a church is the pastor. Right or wrong, we ascribe expectations to this role because of the title. He is the one up front. He is the person with the office and the authority, yet there is often a power broker in the congregation. Sometimes he is on the deacon board. Sometimes he silently functions as the godfather figure. Everyone looks for his nod of approval before taking a position. This individual has often been responsible for hiring or firing a pastor. He controls in spite of his lack of position.

On a more positive side, it is possible for anyone in the church to be a leader. Anyone who has the moral character will emerge as the "go to" person when there are serious issues at stake. The young married couple with relational challenges will seek out those who demonstrate a healthy marriage. The person who evangelizes will automatically be viewed as a spiritual parent. The individual who genuinely cares for others will be elevated as an example. The effective teacher will be given a class. The proactive servant will be recognized.

This principle twists the entire paradigm of how things get done. This is the first lesson from my village in Africa: *Leadership is not a position.*

2

KING OF THE JUNGLE

Learning to lead

*And what you have heard from me in the presence of
many witnesses entrust to faithful men
who will be able to teach others also.*
2 Timothy 2:2

A leader who does not take advice is not a leader.
Kenyan proverb

There is a reason he is called the king of the jungle. Lions are the second largest cat on the planet (after tigers), and they have no predators. They call the shots in the bush veld. None in the animal kingdom thinks otherwise. They are the premier predator of the African savannah. Everything else stays clear and preferably out of sight.

Here is the question: Were they born that way or did they learn to lead? Did they fight their way up the food chain or are they just born leaders? The answer is yes. Both are true.

There is a difference between the newborn of the predators and the prey. Lions are considered *altricial* (helpless) when they are born. On the other hand, antelope, zebra, and other herbivores are *precocial*. That means that within minutes of their birth they are up and walking—even running. This is especially important because the young are often the target of hunting lions. Their strategy is to cull out the weakest of the herd for dinner. Thus the baby wildebeest had better be running within a few minutes of birth.

Lions start off life rather vulnerable. Two weeks pass before they even open their eyes. Though the lioness keeps them hidden from other lions for the first couple months, two thirds of lion cubs do not make it to their first birthday. Life starts out rather tenuously.

So how does this fragile feline become the king of the jungle—the most feared of the animal kingdom? The answer is training. When the cubs are three months old, the lioness begins mentoring them to hunt and kill. Since they can only sprint for short distances, they stalk their prey. Then they pounce. The mother takes the lead, shows them how, and then lets them try. It is through training that lions learn to lead.

At one year of age, the males are kicked out of the pride and must fend for themselves. They are not yet efficient hunters by that time, but there is no choice. It's hunt or die. They may attach themselves to another family of lions, and the learning continues. But ultimately, they learn to lead.

At the same time, they have the DNA of jungle dominance. They are born with the attributes that will eventually allow them to lead. The two-week-old cub is just cuddly, but it is a frightening experience to stand face-to-face with an adult lion.

Which is it? Are leaders born, or can anyone learn to be a leader?

Like the lion, we are born with the DNA of leadership, but most of us need the training. There is a very small number of people who innately know how to lead. It seems that they start calling the shots from the cradle, but the majority of us need equipping, mentoring, and encouragement to succeed.

The premise of this chapter is that there are born leaders, but everyone can learn to lead. Everyone is going to lead someone. The only question is "How many will you lead?" A mother may lead two of her children, while a president of a corporation may lead ten thousand. Both are leaders. Both can be trained to lead better. While some may seem to do it naturally, the rest of us can learn. The rest of us had better learn.

There is a theological reason for learning to lead that extends into the next life. Believers will reign with Christ (2 Timothy 2:12). One of the functions of Christians in the next life is to provide leadership for others (Matthew 25:14-30; Luke 19:11-27). Right now we get to practice for a heavenly job. At some point in eternity we will have further leadership responsibilities. Now is the time to prove our trustworthiness and to be vetted for our role in the next life.

There is also a practical reason why we need to learn more about leadership. The leader is the lid. A leader's leadership abilities limit those who are following. It caps the potential of the organization he leads. Whatever organization or people you lead will rise no higher than you. In case you missed it: THE LEADER IS THE LID.

A leader must come to grips with the fact that he is the limiting factor for the organization. Why does a computer company like Apple thrive while other computer companies fail? They all have access to the same technology, the same market, and the same knowledge base. The difference is leadership.

Once a leader admits that he is the problem, he can then seek help to be better than he is right now. That comes through coaching and mentoring. Every leader needs someone to help him lift the lid off his own limitations. You owe it to those you lead to do better tomorrow than you did today.

Until recently, leadership was not part of the normal curriculum in ministry training institutions like Bible colleges or seminaries. That seems rather strange, since pastors and missionaries are required to lead. There was much emphasis on exegesis and homiletics. Theology dominated the curriculum. Yet very little attention was given to learning about leadership. At best we watched the college president in action, but even that was not always a transferable model in other kinds of ministry.

Fortunately, this has changed. Leadership courses are increasingly part of the requirements for graduation. A three-hour course in seminary is still not sufficient to equip a leader. Be encouraged—there are several things you can do.

Watch Leaders. Become a "groupie." Take advantage of every opportunity to be around leaders. Shine their shoes, carry their briefcases, do anything that will allow you to spend time with leaders.

One of the first leaders that impacted me as a role model was Bill Rudd, the youth pastor of the church I attended in my senior year of high school. He was there when I came home for Christmas and summer vacations from college. As I left and went into ministry, multiple times I would be faced with a decision about how to move forward. One question would often come to mind: How would Bill do this? Having a real live role model enables a leader to sift through the options and do things with excellence.

Our flight was delayed from an African country. We were all crowded into a small departure lounge with standing room only. The delay was due to a traffic jam outside the airport, and the pilot couldn't get to the terminal. An overseas visitor became obnoxious with loud complaints to ground crew who had no control over the situation. Then he got on his cell phone to complain to the airline. Increasingly, he made the other passengers uncomfortable and irate.

From ten feet away, I watched a businessman in an impeccable suit take charge of the situation. He engaged the offensive traveler with firm, direct communication. Over the next few minutes this businessman turned this obtuse traveler into a friend. They were exchanging business cards and pleasantries while boarding the plane. I learned some lessons that day about handling difficult people. Those lessons could not be taught in a classroom. Watching a leader in action was the best way to learn.

Read about leaders. The first and most important text for reading about leadership is biographies in the Bible. The most well-known Bible stories are also lessons of leadership. In addition to that, there are thousands of books written on the topic. Whatever you establish as a reading plan, make sure that at least 25 percent of those books are biographies.

The despots and dictators of the world were also leaders, but they were stark examples of what not to do. Many of the most famous leaders in the Christian world had major flaws. Those negative examples will help to solidify a philosophy of leadership. One of the amazing things about the Bible is that it speaks openly about both the strengths and the weaknesses of leaders. Many great leaders also had great flaws, and the Bible reports that too. A reason to read their stories is to find both positive and negative examples.

Read leadership books. This is different from reading biographies, the life stories of leaders. There is another genre of authors who write about the subject of leadership. Amazon lists over 80,000 books on the topic. Google the word *leadership* and the selection surfaces more than 500 million resources. That makes me question my sanity in writing another book on the same topic. Most of the secular books and many of the "Christian" books on the topic of leadership are not Bible-based. Let the buyer beware.

One of the keys to critical discernment of books about leadership is to separate leadership theory from leadership tools. The basic presuppositions of leadership theory are based on either Scripture or someone's worldview. Our natural disposition should be to look with suspicion at anything man creates. His fallen nature taints and skews his view of the world.

On the other hand, there are many tricks of the trade that are merely tools of the trade. There are useful time management tips that make us efficient and effective. There are time management tools that streamline our day. Speech training will help any leader to communicate more effectively and thus impact others. The digital world has provided dozens of organizational tools that can help us manage the complexities of our job. Team building tips and techniques can help us serve others better. The list is endless.

So read books about leadership. But be sure to identify what is leadership theory and what is a leadership tool.

Seek a mentor. I stumbled onto this concept. My first term on the mission field was a time of floundering. Even though I had completed Bible College and worked as an assistant pastor, I was not ready to be a missionary. Those first years confirmed that. It was during the second term in South Africa that God brought Marc Blackwell into my life. We never signed any contracts or made formal mentoring agreements. We just did it. Marc was with another agency and a few years older and many ministry miles ahead of me. Our relationship enabled me to leap-frog forward at twice the speed of self-learning.

At the root of these four suggestions is the presupposition that a leader must be a life-long learner. It is assumed that no one is at the top of his game. No one is the best he can be. That means the leader is always looking for someone a few steps ahead from whom he can learn. The leader is constantly seeking to improve. Every year, part of his goals will be to do something to increase leadership capacity. It shows up in the job description. It is something in the budget. It is calendared. It is a priority.

The Apostle Paul was an incredible example of life-long learning. He was sitting in a dungeon about to face death. He knew his days were numbered—the sentence of death had already been passed. He could almost hear the footsteps of the executioner. In that setting he was writing his last letter, the book of 2 Timothy. In spite of his impending death he writes: *Bring the books and the parchments.* He was a student right to the end. The rattle of chains, the dank air, and the poor lighting were not conducive to learning. Those were minor problems compared to the foreboding fear of beheading. In spite of all this, Paul wanted to keep learning.

An insatiable appetite to improve is key to leading. It is sad to be around adults who have stopped learning. Conversation is mundane. Life is in neutral. It is only a matter of time before their leadership capital will be spent. Henry Ford put it this way: "Anyone who stops learning is old, whether twenty or eighty. Anyone who keeps learning stays young."[4]

During my college years, I was introverted. There was no one more insecure on campus. It affected me socially and thwarted my leadership potential. My shyness was interpreted as aloofness. I was a social dwarf.

I cannot forget my first preaching opportunity in a real live church situation. The little church I was attending during Bible College invited me to speak. For the month before that assignment, I was physically sick with the dread and anticipation of standing before a small group. Joan, my fiancée, was in the congregation that night and heard my first message. She later confessed that she wrote to her parents and said, "I really like this guy, but he'll never be a preacher." After that message, I started exploring other career paths. There was no way I could be a preacher and leader. My role was most certainly the back seat, not the platform.

My story is proof that those who are not born leaders can be trained. Never could I have imagined that I would be leading a mission organization. Thousands of audiences and sermons later, I'm doing what I never would have dreamed for myself. The key is that I have been a student of leadership over the years and proven that it is possible to overcome deficiencies of birth.

Many leaders began life looking like they would not amount to much. It is reported that Winston Churchill was a slacker who preferred the confines of a bar rather than a library. He was cynical and appeared foolish. Albert Einstein was deemed a mediocre student at best. He was known more for his anti-social behavior than for brilliance of mind. Helen

Keller acted more like an animal than a human being. Yet she graduated from college with honors, having conquered five languages, and completely changed the world's perception of the potential of those who are deaf and blind. The list of high profile leaders who started off badly is almost endless.

You too may view yourself as a defenseless, blind lion cub with no leadership potential. But roar! You can be king of some leadership jungle. Now would be a good time to learn how to lead.

3

LORRIES

Paradigm shifts

. . . men who had understanding of the times.
1 Chronicles 12:32

*In the moment of crisis, the wise build bridges
and the foolish build dams.*
Nigerian proverb

I was born in Des Moines, Iowa, while my parents were in the United States between assignments in Nigeria. I was four months old when our family boarded a ship in New York harbor with a four-wheel-drive jeep. After arriving in Lagos, Nigeria, we headed up country. The destination was Gadaka. The road ended before we got there. In true pioneering spirit, Dad kept right on going. Through the savannah he pushed on until he arrived at the village that would be my first home.

One of his first jobs was to build a temporary shelter that consisted of a tent and a couple grass shacks. The next phase was a two-bedroom home made of adobe brick that was whitewashed inside and out. In the process of frequent trips back to the nearest town for supplies and mail, he created a "road." Part of the distance was just two tracks, but over time a recognizable dirt road appeared. For the first time in history, this remote village had motor vehicle access to the outside world.

It was not long until the lorries came to town. (*Lorry* is the British word for truck.) This "road" opened a corridor of transportation that had never existed. At the time, Nigeria was a British colony, so English words found their way into village vocabulary.

English jargon brought a level of sophistication to our village. It became popular to use English words. A mother gave birth to a child and named him Torchlight (the British word for flashlight). She gave birth again and the second child was named Batteries. Western civilization had arrived in our village.

But I digress. Back to the lorries. These were three-ton trucks with eight-foot sidewalls on the back. They carried incredible loads—way beyond any manufacturer's recommendation or imagination. Cargo filled the back while passengers perched precariously on top. Each truck had a driver and his partner who was called a *karen mota*. The driver was a rock star, a cut above everyone else. He would swing down from the cab of the truck and then swagger off to let lower mortals deal with the mundane responsibilities of loading and unloading.

For a ten-year-old boy in Africa, the *karen mota* was my hero. He was sort of like the conductor on a train. As second in command, he was in charge of everything and everyone on the truck. Passengers paid their fares to the *karen mota*. He would oversee the loading of cargo. He was large and in charge. But the best thing about the *karen mota* was that he always seemed to be preoccupied with other business as the lorry started to pull out of town. He would then run after the lorry and, without missing a step, swing himself up onto the back of it. He rode hanging onto the back and over the side. He was cool. As a kid, I wanted to be the *karen mota*.

The lorries created a major paradigm shift. No longer was this a village cut off from outside civilization. All the conveniences and products of the world were now accessible. Every village had a market day. Ours was held on Sunday.

Early in the morning, the lorries would start rumbling into town and unloading. The entire population would gather at the central market to talk, gawk, and possibly purchase something.

For hundreds of years, market day consisted of vegetables, homemade clay pots, gourds, colorful fabrics, and herbal medicines. With the advent of lorries there were radios, batteries, flashlights, candy, and plastic buckets. Market day had a completely different feel to it.

This was a paradigm shift. Our village came out of the dark ages in a matter of months. The items in the market profoundly affected the way life had been lived in this village for many generations.

A paradigm is simply a model, a way of looking at things. It is "the way we do things around here." A paradigm shift is a basic change in assumptions. It is a change from one way of thinking to another. It could be a revolution or a more subtle metamorphosis. But things are now different. The rules have changed. The previous worldview has been shattered, and there are new ways of seeing the universe. A paradigm shift results in naming your child Torchlight or Battery, which breaks the tradition of hundreds of years of naming children Bulus or Musa.

Some of the more obvious paradigm shifts of history were things like the discovery of fire, the use of metal instruments, the invention of the printing press, the shift from horse and buggy to automobile, and the telegraph to the Internet. Each of these had a profound impact on culture and society. They completely changed the world. Stone arrowheads were swapped for metal. Books became available to the masses. Cars created a mobile society. The Internet shrunk the world.

Kodak is in the news as I write this chapter. The company is in danger of going out of business. This never could have been imagined thirty years ago. It dominated the film industry. Other companies nibbled around the edges but Kodak was the giant. The paradigm shift to digital cameras brought down this "invincible" company. Once digital photography took over, there was no reason for 35mm film.

Being aware of paradigm shifts is often what makes or breaks a leader. The ability to forecast the future and recognize and capitalize on shifting paradigms is a basic skill of a leader. Leaders spend their time thinking about the future. It is their job to be looking at the horizon. The person who sees the furthest is often the leader. Anticipation is a key component to the making of a leader. Understanding paradigm shifts gives the leader a head start.

Gretzky, the great hockey player, said he simply anticipated where the puck would be and skated there.[5] That is what leaders do. New leaders emerge simply because they know where the puck is going.

Leaders are those who see things differently. They look at the same problem everyone else observes but see potential where others see problems. This is a foundational leadership skill. How often have you said, "I should have seen that one coming"? Someone other than you probably did. That is why he is the leader.

The biblical *Sons of Issachar* illustrate this principle. Scripture says that they were *men who had understanding of the times, to know what Israel ought to do* (I Chronicles 12:32). These were men who grasped what was happening around them. Things were changing. They were in tune with those changes. That gave them the ability to make good decisions and guide the nation of Israel in the right direction.

One of the major paradigm shifts in the Bible was the transition from the Old Testament to the New Testament. The mental model before Jesus arrived was that you had to be a Jew to connect with God. That was a playing field with high walls. These barriers kept Gentiles away. Most could not see any other approach.

Along came the Apostle Paul. Jesus had already said there would be people following Him from every nation on earth. Paul put feet to that paradigm shift. He knew that Gentiles could be part of God's family. The Jews almost crucified Him for that idea, but His persistence brought about a massive expansion of the church that is still reverberating 2000 years later. He was able to break out of the mental model that only Jews could be saved. That is what made Him a leader.

Einstein said, "We can't solve problems by using the same kind of thinking we used when we created them."[6] The leader is a person who is able to see beyond the current paradigm and moves things forward. Einstein also said, "The only thing that interferes with my learning is my education."[7] While we value higher learning, it can sometimes be a trap that limits our ability to lead. The paradigms we learned in school may be cement boots that hinder forward progress.

If others have a head start in your industry, it is difficult to break in and succeed. Everyone else has a lot more experience and momentum, and you will struggle to compete. Here is the exciting dynamic of a paradigm shift, however: the playing field is leveled. Once the paradigm shift takes place, everyone is on equal footing. It is new game with a new set of rules. You now have a chance to play where only the big boys previously dominated.

During the Industrial Era of American history, there was no way for a Mark Zuckerberg to lead a multi-billion-dollar company at twenty-seven years old. CEOs were company men in their fifties who had climbed the corporate ladder. The Internet brought a whole new game to town. Now a college kid could start Facebook and capture the participation of 250 million people. That would never have happened before the paradigm shift that was brought on by the invention of the Internet.

In a profound paradigm shift, this is the first generation that does not depend on authority figures for information. It is difficult to know whom to credit for that observation. Think of that. Since the creation of the world, people have gone to kings, priests, and academia to obtain information. The Internet leveled this playing field.

Wiki has emboldened everyone to see himself or herself as an authority. The result is that college students Google during class to compare the thoughts of others while the professor lectures. No longer does a person in authority have authority. This can be intimidating to those with the position. On the other hand, think of the incredible potential when people are not limited to one mental model.

The Apostle Paul was headed to Rome as a prisoner when the ship got to an island just before the end of the sailing season. It wasn't an attractive place to spend the winter, so the captain decided to sail on. His rationale is given in Acts 27:13. *Now when the south wind blew gently, supposing that they had obtained their purpose, they weighed anchor and sailed.* That trip ended in disaster because the captain misjudged the signs. The gentle winds were misleading, and he failed to read the circumstances.

There are multiple responses to impending storms. Some leaders do nothing. They see the storm clouds gathering but keep sailing like nothing is changing. Other leaders become more controlling and sail faster, right into disaster. Yet other leaders make tentative and insipid adjustments to their course that are not sufficient to miss the hurricane. A fourth approach is to throw stuff overboard. These leaders jettison cargo in the forms of programs, property, and budget priorities in order to save the ship. Another approach is simply to jump ship . . . resign.

It takes great wisdom to adjust to the winds of change. Some leaders intuitively know what is happening. They see the indicators nibbling away at the edges of the present paradigm. They almost have a sixth sense.

Not all leaders have that intuition, but they can still navigate well if they listen to others. These "advisors" are often the mavericks or novices or eccentrics—sometimes even prisoners in chains like Paul. These people are not marching with the rest of the crowd. They may not be leaders and may not do much with their observations, but they are a source for understanding what is over the horizon.

The motto for Luxembourg is, "We wish to remain as we are." That saying is chiseled in granite on walls in the city. Some view change as a dirty word. Not only Luxembourgers hold to that thought. Many of us have that same slogan etched in our heads.

Someone has said, "We don't mind change; we just don't want to be changed." The irony is that leaders are some of the most resistant to change. They want others to change but will not embrace it themselves. Ultimately there cannot be forward progress if there is no change. If the scenery is not changing, you are standing still. Bringing about change is the role of leaders.

I was visiting in Argentina and my host told me the following story. He said a holy man and his assistant were walking in the Andes Mountains and came to the hut of a peasant. Their poverty was stark. Their only possession of value was a milk cow. After visiting with these poverty-stricken people, the holy man proceeded down the path. After a while, he told his assistant to go back and push the cow over the side of the mountain. The assistant obeyed but lived with remorse for treating this peasant family so badly.

A year later the assistant could not stand the guilt any longer and headed up the mountain to apologize and make restitution. As he rounded the corner, he viewed a mansion where the one-room hut had been located. He obviously thought he was in the wrong place until the peasant came out and insisted that they indeed were the peasants he had visited the previous year.

"What happened?" asked the holy man's assistant. "Well, our cow fell off the mountain," answered the peasant, "so we had to find another way to make a living. We discovered that the tourists down in the city love our woven blankets. We started a factory that now employs seventy-five people, and we are incredibly wealthy beyond our dreams."

Sometimes the best thing to do is push some sacred cows over the cliff. It seems cruel. It leaves us without any resources or plans. But often the paradigm shift is the best thing that can happen to us. It causes us to think in new ways and see new opportunities. Leaders agonize over getting rid of sacred cows. But sometimes it is the best thing a leader can do.

There is risk associated with leading change during a paradigm shift. Someone has said that you can tell who the pioneers are—they are the ones with arrows in their backs. Settlers show up later when it is a little safer. Settlers are not leaders—pioneers are. They arrived there first but paid a price for doing it. They are the ones who find the new worlds. They are the ones who go down in history for leading the way.

One of the key responsibilities of leaders is to look into the future. There are tremendous opportunities coming that have never been imagined. Leadership demands a discerning eye and a bold heart to steer in the right direction.

So . . . what lorries are coming to your town?

4

MAI HAJI

The importance of vision

*. . . forgetting what lies behind and
straining forward to what lies ahead.*
Philippians 3:13

Before shooting, one must aim.
African proverb

U ntil my dad built a road to Gadaka, the villagers lived in vehicular isolation from the rest of the world. When the lorries came to town, something happened. This sparked the entrepreneurial spirit of one man who began dreaming of owning a lorry.

That is vision. He saw possibilities that others did not. The rest of the villagers were excited about the plastic trinkets hauled in by the lorries from the outside world. Mai Haji was excited about the possibility of possessing the lorry that delivered the trinkets. He was no different from anyone else in town—except he had vision.

In its most basic form, vision is simply seeing what could be possible in the future. The rest of the villagers were content to hoe their gardens, own a couple goats, and periodically have chicken with their cornmeal porridge. But not Mai Haji. Status quo was not acceptable. He imagined things bigger and better. He was a leader. Having vision distinguished him from the crowd.

Thomas Huxley was a disciple of Darwin, a biologist and a self-avowed humanist living at the end of the 19th Century. He was lecturing one day in Dublin, Ireland, and went over the allotted time. Realizing he was late for his next appointment, he ran out of the lecture hall and jumped into his waiting horse-drawn carriage. "Hurry, I'm late. Drive fast!" he shouted to the driver.

Obedient to his employer, the driver cracked his whip and the carriage was soon careening through the streets of the city. A few minutes into the wild ride, Huxley realized he had forgotten to tell the driver of his next destination. Leaning out the window he shouted, "Do you know where you are going?" To which the driver shouted back, "No, Your Honor, but we sure are going fast, aren't we?"[8]

Many in the Western world live like that. Life is fast-paced. We careen through the streets of our lives without much thought of the destination. Ultimately there is one simple issue that makes a leader a leader. He knows where he is going. Followers meander through life without a destination in mind. Leaders race with an eye for a goal. They have vision.

A visionary is one who is constantly looking over the horizon to tomorrow. He or she understands that figuring out the next step is a primary responsibility of a leader. I have summarized my own job as "articulating and activating the vision." A defining quality of leaders is the capacity to create and implement a vision.

Some have joked about the Christopher Columbus School of Management. "When he left, he didn't know where he was going; when he got there, he didn't know where he was; and when he got back, he couldn't tell them where he had been." But the reality was that he did have vision. This was a time in history when the earth was thought to be flat. The mapmakers simply wrote on the edges: "Beyond, there be dragons."

But Columbus saw what might be possible and pushed beyond the charts. That is leadership. Seneca, the Roman Stoic philosopher, put it another way: "If a man knows not what harbor he seeks, any wind is the right direction."[9] Columbus sailed against the wind of popular opinion, and we are still talking about him 500 years later.

Hyrum W. Smith put it this way: "A goal is a planned conflict with the status quo."[10] It is the ability to move beyond the norm. It is the capacity to see potential. It is a Mai Haji who can envision a fleet of lorries.

I learned something about vision from my son. After one excursion on a friend's sailboat, he went out and bought one. "How hard can it be?" was indicative of his optimistic and visionary spirit. One of the amazing lessons from sailing is that you go faster by sailing into the wind.

Conventional wisdom would instruct you to put the wind to your back and sail with it. The problem with that is you can only go as fast as the wind is blowing. When you tack into the wind, you actually pick up speed. The sail acts like the wing on an airplane. The airflow over the top literally sucks the plane up into the air. Rotate that same "wing" into a vertical position and you have a sail that does the same thing—it pulls the boat forward at a pace faster than the wind is blowing.

That is what vision does—it pulls you forward. Followers set their sails to go with prevailing opinions. Leaders head into the wind, against the norm, and into the storm. An amazing thing happens. Heading in a different direction actually propels them forward at a faster and more exhilarating pace. That is why "conflict with the status quo" is so critical to leadership.

There has never been anyone more visionary than Jesus. He made the following brash statement: *You will be my witnesses in Jerusalem and in all Judea and Samaria, and to the end of the earth* (Acts 1:8). He was speaking to eleven, rough-hewn, uneducated, fearful men. They had failed Him. They didn't seem to get the lessons of the past three years of discipleship. Yet, Jesus envisioned a worldwide impact. That was an incredible statement for a man who rarely stepped out of the border of his own country. Now, two thousand years later, that vision has been accomplished. The gospel has reached around the globe.

Obviously, we can't speak with the same certainty about the future, but Jesus could because He was deity. We can't. So all of our plans for the future must be flavored by the spirit of James 4:13-17—*if the Lord wills.* Any planning that excludes God is arrogant, or at the best, naïve. James was speaking of a merchant who was an achiever. He saw business opportunities in a new market and planned to capitalize on it for the next year. His bottom-line objective was the bottom line. James called him a fool and pleads for humility in planning. But he does not say don't plan. His warning was against living life independently from God. The instruction was to plan—but make sure all plans are written in pencil—acknowledging that God has an eraser.

Jesus urged his followers to be planners. He taught what it meant to follow Him (Luke 14:25-33). His standards were demanding. Right in the middle of this discussion, Jesus stopped to give two parables. The first was about a man who wanted to build a tower but had not done a cost analysis. Halfway through the project he discovered he could not finish it. The second illustration was about a king who was considering going to war. He sent out scouts to let him know whether or not he was outnumbered. If so, he knew to send an ambassador instead of an army.

The point of both of those parables is to plan ahead. Setting goals is part of being a follower of Jesus. After these two illustrations Christ went right back to discussing what it meant to be His disciple. It is obvious that Jesus thought His followers should plan.

The Apostle Paul was a planner. He was always thinking about the future. A classic passage that illustrates this is found in his letter to the Romans. In chapter 15 he writes about his vision to preach the gospel where it had never been presented before. His target area was from Jerusalem to Illyricum. That is a swath of land that extends from Israel through Turkey and Greece and all the way up to Croatia.

This plan limited his endeavors, and that was a good thing. In this letter to the Romans he indicates that up until that point he could not come visit them because he was focused on his vision. Having goals limits the leader. It is good to have boundaries. Paul couldn't be everywhere, so he decided on his "somewhere." Having those boundaries helped him to say no to good things. One of the benefits of having a plan for the future is that it becomes a grid for decision-making. There are always far more opportunities than can be addressed. Having a vision for the future helps the leader stay focused.

My son got involved in motocross racing. I stood watching mud-covered contestants scream past. Along came some old guy that just seemed to be puttering along. Since I rode motorcycles in my younger days, it was obvious that I could compete with those old guys. Ryan wisely suggested that I might want to practice a little before entering my first race. What a disaster!

It was soon obvious that the thirty years that separated me from my last motorcycle ride had taken its toll. I had never been so tired in my life after this practice round. Most of my time was spent getting back on the bike and trying to kick-start the engine. That motorcycle just didn't seem to stay on the path. It was then that my son gave me an important lesson in leadership: Look at where you want to go, not where you are right now.

He was exactly right. As I navigated along a narrow ledge or past a stream or through some ruts, I had been concentrating on not going there—but inevitably did. Once I started looking further ahead at my destination and quit worrying about the bumps in the road, it radically changed my ability to stay on the bike.

Alice came to a crossroad in her journey to Wonderland. The Cheshire Cat asked where she was going. Alice's answer was that she didn't really know. The cat's perceptive response was "then it doesn't matter which path you take." Leaders without vision are merely drifters.

Keeping your eyes on a destination on the horizon helps to absorb the bumps along the way. The skier on the mountainside gets down the hill because his knees act like shock absorbers to respond to the unevenness of the slope. The effective leader does not become overwhelmed with today's problems. Yes, he has to flex but blows on past the obstacle toward the goal. Yes, problems must be fixed, but the good leader realizes that challenges along the way are mere annoyances, not obstacles. A good leader adjusts to the bumps in the road and then gets back to the race.

One of our family traditions is to work on a 1000- or 2000-piece puzzle at Thanksgiving and Christmas. A table is dedicated to the joint project as people come and go. The first step before working on the puzzle is to look at the cover of the box. It is a lot easier to put the pieces in the right place if you can see the completed picture first. That is what vision does. It gives a clear picture of success.

The job of the leader is first to paint that picture. Then as people join the effort, they know exactly what they are working toward. There are multiple benefits that come from having a vision for the future.

It creates motivation. It is rather difficult to be excited about doing nothing unless you are on vacation. Even then, we want to do something. Vision motivates action. There is no excitement in kicking a ball around. But put that same ball on a soccer field with goal posts on each end and 80,000 people all of a sudden become energized. Living life with no goals is boring.

It creates unity. The reason a sports team works together is because each participant wants the same thing. Put those same people in another setting and unity dissipates. A goal creates unity. The players on the soccer team may have nothing to do with each other off the field, but blow the whistle to start the game and there is instant unity. One of the reasons for disunity in churches and organizations is the lack of a unified goal. It is no wonder churches have internal struggles when everyone is heading in a different direction. Get people pulling in the same direction and they will not be so concerned about the oddities of the person next to them.

It creates focus. Having a single goal eliminates a multitude of other options. One of the challenges of life is determining priorities. Goals have the capacity to narrow the list of options. There is no question on the soccer team that everyone needs to focus on the 8 x 24-foot rectangle at the end of the field. It doesn't matter what is happening in the stands or on the sidelines. Having a goal directs energy to one destination.

It creates a target. Imagine the chaos if every member on the soccer team chose his own goal. It would be impossible to play the game. It would be even more difficult to win a game. The role of leadership is to define the goal and make sure everyone knows where it is.

There are many formulas and acronyms for setting goals. In the spirit of the simplicity of my village in Africa, I'll forgo those. Instead, just pick a mountain peak on the horizon and head in that direction.

The takeaway from Mai Haji is simply to dream about the future. Have one big idea out there and start working toward it. This simple man from a remote village in Africa had no idea about mechanics, business plans, or spread sheets. He simply knew he wanted to own a lorry. Having that vision gave him purpose. It created energy and risk-taking. He became focused. Ultimately, he became a leader.

So . . . what is your lorry?

5

ANTHILLS

The art of teamwork

*For the body does not consist of one member
but of many.*
1 Corinthians 12:14

*If you want to go quickly, go alone.
If you want to go far, go together.*
African proverb

One of my fond memories of childhood growing up in northeastern Nigeria was climbing anthills. These mountains of dirt are amazing. The tallest ever found was 40 feet tall and 10 feet across. Building it meant that ants had moved 40 tons of dirt by a coordinated effort. It took more than a million of them. Incredible! Especially when little creatures smaller than a half inch in length did it.

The most impressive part of an anthill doesn't show. This is a typical iceberg situation where the majority of the structure is below the surface. Super colonies can extend laterally for more than 50 miles. These ant-cities are a building feat that proportionately compares with the Great Wall of China in magnitude. Some of the larger colonies have an estimated 300 million ants.

These insects are organized. There is soldier-like order. Tunnel systems connect room after room, each with its own purpose. Some rooms store food. Others are for hatching eggs, mating, and nurseries. Others are resting places for the worker ants. The queen has her own private quarters. No chaos. Teamwork is built into their culture and DNA. A sophisticated ventilation system keeps the temperature at 87 degrees regardless of the African weather outside.

Ants call these structures home, but people have used them for many other purposes. The trekkers (African pioneers) turned them into ovens by carving out a space in the middle, building a wood fire, and cooking their food.

Others have used this clay composite to make bricks, thus eliminating the need to dig deep for building materials. During famine times, Africans have been known to dig into these anthills to find the seed stores placed there by the ants. Gold miners have dug into these mounds to find flecks of gold brought to the surface by these industrious termites, thus locating veins of gold.

All this happens by team effort. These towers of dirt are formed one grain at a time by the combined effort of millions of ants. There is one word for this: TEAMWORK.

Two passages of Scripture talk about the lowly ant:

Go to the ant, O sluggard; consider her ways, and be wise. Without having any chief, officer, or ruler, she prepares her bread in summer and gathers her food in harvest (Proverbs 6:6-8).

Four things on earth are small, but they are exceedingly wise: the ants are a people not strong, yet they provide their food in the summer (Proverbs 30:24-25).

Both passages point us to the industrious nature of ants. They work together as a team to accomplish great feats. They plan ahead. They almost never sleep and are constantly foraging for food or digging new tunnels. They work together to thrive and survive.

Ants are incredibly ambitious. I can remember leaving a piece of wood on the ground at night in Africa. The next morning the entire 2 x 4 was covered with ant tunnels. While I slept, they worked. They worked together. No single ant could have accomplished that. They are the epitome of teamwork and industry.

The observation of Solomon in Proverbs is that ants don't have an organizational chart. They just work together. No captain, overseer, or ruler is needed to make this teamwork happen. Ants are one of the few social insects in the world. While much of the rest of the insect world flies solo, ants live and work together as a colony. They live for the sake of others. When they find food, they bring it back to be stored and shared. As they head back to the nest, they leave a chemical trail behind them so others can find their way to the food source. Everything is done in a choreographed manner that serves each other.

Wonderful things happen when people work in teams. Biblical Ministries Worldwide adopted the following definition of team and teamwork. In our minds there is a difference.

A Team consists of a group of people in a common location with common interests who support one another in the ministry but who do not work on a common project.

TeamWORK is the process whereby a group of people must collaborate on a common project, utilizing their diversity of gifts, to accomplish a greater goal that would be *impossible to achieve without collaboration.*

The operative word is *collaboration*. If a person is able to fulfill a job by himself, there is no need for teamwork. The individual might be part of a larger vision and thus a member of a loosely defined team. He may have specific goals for himself. If he doesn't need anyone else around to complete the vision and goals, he doesn't need teamwork.

Acts 20:4 is one of those verses we normally skip over. We certainly don't memorize verses like this. But each verse of Scripture is inspired of God and has purpose. This verse screams out TEAMWORK.

Sopater the Berean, son of Pyrrhus, accompanied him; and of the Thessalonians, Aristarchus and Secundus; and Gaius of Derbe, and Timothy; and the Asians, Tychicus and Trophimus.

This is a list of Paul the Apostle's team at this specific time in his missionary journey. He never operated without a team. His first missionary journey was with Barnabas and John Mark. His second journey started off with Silas and soon added Timothy. We are aware of forty-one different team members with Paul at various times during his ministry. He was constantly interacting with them. Sometimes he would go ahead and wait for them. Other times he sent them on assignments. At times they took a boat and he walked. Ultimately, the Apostle Paul was committed to working in a team.

We tend to put Paul on a pedestal. He gets most of the credit for all the churches established in those early days. The reality is that it happened because of teamwork.

The word *synergy* carries the idea of greater results because of combined efforts. If it was defined in mathematical terms, it would be 1+1 = 3. That doesn't work in math but it does in teamwork. Geese fly in a *V* formation because flying together enables them to add 70 percent more distance using the same energy. A single draft horse can pull 4000 pounds, but when 2 are harnessed together they can pull 12,000 pounds. A flimsy piece of veneer is easily broken, but when laminated with others it forms plywood.

The Bible speaks of this principle. *Five of you shall chase a hundred, and a hundred of you shall chase ten thousand* (Leviticus 26:8). There are exponential results where there is the synergy of teamwork. This is at the heart of teamwork. There is much greater potential if we link arms.

Most people have never participated on an effective team. Those who have done so speak in glowing terms as they recount the experience. It is a beautiful thing when it works like an African ant colony. It is distressing when it doesn't. There are basically two reasons why teams become dysfunctional.

1. Spiritual issues - When a team has problems, someone is probably not acting like Jesus. It could be any number of sins that rise to the top—selfishness, anger, graceless communication, lack of prayer, or pride. Ultimately, there is probably sin in the equation. Someone is more interested in self than in others.

2. Skill issues - There are some basic things every team needs to know and do in order to function well. Dysfunction is not always an indicator that people are acting in a sinful manner. They may just not be aware of the dynamics of a team.

It is possible for a spiritually minded team to have difficulties simply because they are unaware of the skills and knowledge needed for participating in a team. Their spirituality can compensate for these inadequacies, but it will still be a tough job.

It is also possible to have the skills and knowledge needed to operate as a team but lack spiritual maturity. Either team could succeed, but combining both skills and spirituality makes for a winning combination.

Teamwork is extremely difficult. There are more failures than successes, and it is often catastrophic when it fails. Relationships are fractured. Bitterness or cynicism may set in. Team members become wary about ever joining another team. The task is not accomplished and goals are not reached. The fallout can affect people for a very long time.

This is a high-risk endeavor, but it is a risk that must be taken.

Nothing can guarantee success. Preparing for teamwork can, however, increase the chances of success. There are basically two components:

1. Appreciating the strengths of each team member. There is value in diversity among team members. If each individual had the same personality and ability, the team could not function well. Someone would be redundant. Yet it is those differences that cause the friction. One of the first steps in forming the team is to speak openly about strengths and weaknesses of each member. This enables everyone to rejoice in each member's contribution and not be frustrated where a member does not excel.

2. Commitment to the other team members. Before a team can begin working on a project together, there are some preliminary questions that should be addressed regarding the members' commitment to each other and to the task. They must first answer four questions: Why? What? Where? and How?

Mission (Why?) - The purpose statement of a team clearly articulates why this team exists. This is the most foundational question. If this cannot be answered, immediately disband the team. There is no reason to proceed. There is no potential for success.

Values (What?) - The core values of a team clearly articulate what is important to this group. Most friction in a team comes because the group is not united about what is most important. Each member may have a different list of values for his or her personal life, but for this specific team, there must be agreement about the core values.

Vision (Where?) - The vision statement of the team clearly articulates where this group is headed. What is the goal? It is possible for a group of people to agree about purpose and values but have no destination in mind. This group will quickly head off in a variety of directions, all the while shouting over their shoulders that the others should follow them. Ultimately, there must be one over-riding goal for the team.

Strategies (How?) - The strategy statement of the team clearly articulates how the team expects to get from "here" to "there." This is where strong-willed people have difficulty. Each person knows best how to get the job done. There may be multiple ways to reach the destination, but ultimately, one of them must be chosen. Everyone must agree on the method and then do it together.

Until these four questions are answered, it is expecting a lot from a team member to commit to anything. But once all four items are on paper, each person can make an objective decision about commitment. This is more than agreement. Commitment calls for a no-retreat mentality with 100 percent effort until the destination is reached.

Ken Blanchard puts it this way: "There's a difference between interest and commitment. When you're interested in something, you do it only when it's convenient. When you're committed to something, you accept no excuses; only results."[11] Once there is commitment from each team member, some mighty large anthills can be built.

My colleague, Dave Brown, missionary in Africa, wrote the following in an email prayer letter:

> There is an amazing phrase I have learned in my studies that captures a core value in the African culture: *umuntu ngmuntu ngbantu* (don't even try to pronounce it). It means "A person is a person through another person." The idea is that we are defined by, and find our significance through, our family and community. No one is independent; we need each other.
>
> Europeans and Americans tend to desire independence and autonomy, but this African value is why millions of orphans aren't dead or in orphanages; the children belong to the village.

Western culture has created complex paradigms for teamwork, but the ant colonies of Africa know how to do it best. We might do well to follow the advice of Solomon, the wisest man in the world: *Go to the ant.*

6

DODO

Define reality

*Have I then become your enemy
by telling you the truth?*
Galatians 4:16

The leader knows the reality.
Kenyan proverb

Thehere were *dodos* (doh-dohs) in one of the Nigerian villages where my parents lived and worked. These are not the flightless birds of the island of Mauritius in the Indian Ocean. They were men of the village who dressed up as spirit men. Their attire was simply made of leaves. Lots of leaves. They looked like round balls of vegetation with only their legs showing, kind of like the trees a little child would draw—a circle with a trunk.

These *dodos* would come out of the hills and parade through the village. They terrorized the villagers, especially the children, as they danced around. Women would scatter. Older men "in the know" would simply be amused. For most of the villagers, these were spirit beings that haunted their village. They were to be feared.

Never mind that these *dodos* were brothers and uncles and fathers of the village. Since the foliage covered their bodies, they were "unknown." I thought it was the best entertainment in town, but the locals were panicked. Their perception was that these were powerful spirit beings from another world.

In another part of Africa where I lived, they had a different version of the same theme. The Zulus believe in the tokoloshe (toh-koh-losh). According to them he is a short, hairy, dwarf-like creature. The European version is a goblin, leprechaun, or fairy. In Africa it is the tokoloshe and he is to be feared. He has powers of life and death, can impregnate women, and spread the HIV virus. He is a mischievous, evil spirit that is normally only seen by children. He makes himself invisible by swallowing a pebble.

One of the precautions taken against the tokoloshe is to elevate beds by putting bricks under each leg. The assumption is that this puts you out of reach of the tokoloshe since he is not tall enough to "get you."

Traditions, fears, and folklore have some semblance of the truth. The problem is how the facts are interpreted. Everyone in the village saw the same *dodo,* but as outsiders we came away with a different understanding. Zulus raise their beds to be out of reach of the tokoloshe because history proved that people died when their beds were low to the ground. Zulus were convinced the tokoloshe was responsible. Could it be that death came from carbon monoxide poisoning because the bed was right next to a fire that sucked the oxygen out of the space? Maybe it wasn't the tokoloshe?

What do *dodos* and tokoloshes have to do with leadership?

Max DuPree, American businessman and writer, is credited with saying: "The first job of a leader is to define reality."[12] This is a profound observation of leadership. A key responsibility of leaders is to interpret what others may see but to do so with brutal honesty and accuracy. The leader cuts through all the fiction and assumptions and lays truth on the table.

Jack Welch was the CEO of GE, the largest company in the world. He repeatedly said, "Deal with the world as it is, not how you'd like it to be."[13] Many leaders think they can impose their will regardless of the facts. They may not like reality. They may not want to accept that things are really bad. But until they face the truth, they cannot lead. Welch was calling for leaders to define reality.

Your car won't start, so you have it towed to the mechanic. Your assumption might be that the battery is dead. His diagnostic shows that the starter is broken. At that point, the mechanic is leading you. He has defined reality. Only then can there be a solution to the problem. That is why DuPree, Napoleon, and Welch are so perceptive in their statements. The person who can define reality becomes the leader. Ultimately, the leader's job is to bring about change, but he must first articulate the truth.

Imagine that you come upon a serious automobile accident. Five cars are a mass of twisted metal in the middle of the highway. Victims are trapped inside, and others are sprawled on the pavement and grass beside the road. Several other cars stop to assist. There are half a dozen strangers looking at this catastrophe.

One person will often emerge as the leader. He is the one who quickly sizes up the situation and starts telling people what to do. He is the one who is objective enough to evaluate the reality that this person is dead, that one needs to be pulled out of a burning car, another one needs mouth-to-mouth resuscitation, and someone needs to call 911. Because he defines reality and articulates it, people follow. He doesn't need a uniform, badge, or position. Just the fact that he articulates reality makes him instantly a leader.

This is one of the primary responsibilities of a counselor. A person's life may be in chaos. The reason he comes to a counselor is to find someone who can articulate the truth. The counselor's first job is to identify the truth. Until there is an accurate diagnosis of the problem, it is not possible to fix it. He must accurately define the problem before he can offer hope.

A popular brainstorming tool is a SWOT analysis. The idea is to get a group of people in a room to face reality. The approach is to list the strengths (S), weaknesses (W), opportunities (O), and threats (T). Then based on this picture of things as they really are, the team can set a strategy to move forward.

The most difficult of these is often W (the weaknesses). It takes complete honesty, transparency, and humility to admit faults. The brainstorming team may be too timid or too polite at this point. That will defeat the purpose. Ultimately the reason this tool is so effective for strategizing is because it forces leaders to define reality.

It is not possible to fix something without an accurate diagnosis. Imagine a doctor treating a foot fungus when the real problem is cancer. In the same way, a leader must diagnose the problems and possibilities.

One of the foundational responsibilities of a leader is to cast vision. Followers look at their feet. Leaders scan the horizon and point to a destination. That occurs because the leader is able to articulate the reality of where they are and give hope for a better future.

The role of the leader is to say, "This is where we are, these are the challenges we face, and here is where we are headed." Imagine the captain of a ship in the Pacific Ocean who thinks he is in the Atlantic Ocean. He cannot possibly pilot a ship to its destination if he lives in the denial of his present location. In the same way, the leader cannot make problems go away by pretending that they don't exist. He must admit the reality of where he is. Wrong assumptions lead to wrong solutions.

Followers know if a leader does not understand reality. It is common for followers to complain that their leader has his head in the clouds. Living in an artificial world undermines the credibility of a leader. It demoralizes followers. It ultimately undermines all potential of leading unless by coercion. People do not want to follow someone out of touch with reality.

The truth often hurts, but ultimately telling the truth is the most loving thing a leader can do. And followers may push back. The Apostle Paul had that problem. In his letter to the Galatian church he said, *Have I then become your enemy by telling you the truth?* (Galatians 4:16).

Jesus ran into the same problem. He told His enemies, *But now you seek to kill me, a man who has told you the truth* (John 8:40). Withholding the truth is unloving and dangerous. There is tremendous potential for success when we face the brutal truth. That is why Jesus said, *You will know the truth and the truth will set you free* (John 8:32).

It takes courage to speak up like Jesus. It would be much more comfortable to maintain the appearance that everything is okay. It is a lot easier to leave things as they are. The leader feels like an intruder when he or she inserts the brutal truth into the situation. But good leadership unveils reality.

Leaders often find themselves in another difficult place. Because of wisdom and previous experience, they can see the path someone is taking will not turn out well for him. If they intrude and point it out, they are rebuffed as meddling. If they do not voice a warning, they are castigated for not saying something earlier. Ultimately, the best leaders blurt out reality—and that is why they can lead.

There are many ways that leaders may fail to acknowledge reality. Here are just a few examples.

- There may be tensions among team members, but the leader merely ignores that cancer in the organization.

- A pastor may see declining numbers of young people attending his church and simply ignore that fact.

- A businessman may see declining revenues but fail to face the balance sheet with cuts in spending which may, in turn, require retiring some employees.

- A missionary may not be seeing any results and simply blames the unresponsive nature of the people with whom he is working.

- A married couple grows increasingly distant and merely goes through the motions of family life for the sake of the children.

- A church may fail to reach its immediate community because of a changing demographic that church members see as undesirable.

- A family continues to spend with disregard to massive credit card debt.

The list is endless. Each of these situations is a failure in leadership. These leaders are just as fanciful as the villagers' *dodos* and tokoloshes.

7

THE FIRST RAIN

Time management

It is not for you to know times [chronos]
or seasons [kairos]
that the Father has fixed by his own authority.
Acts 1:7

To run is not necessarily to arrive.
Swahili proverb

Rain on a corrugated iron roof is my favorite way to fall asleep at night. It was our version of white noise in the village of Gadaka. Skip the sleeping pills. The quiet roar of raindrops on steel soothes like waves of an ocean.

Our village was located on the edge of the Sahara desert. While the sand dunes were many miles away, the climate was semi-arid. Each year the desert eased toward us a few more feet. That made life difficult for an agrarian society. Without crops, these people would die. There was no other industry to fall back on if there was crop failure. Having food to eat in the dry season depended on successful farming in the wet season.

Dry season meant exactly that—DRY. Not one drop of rain for half the year. All vegetation went brown. Harmattan is dust that rolls in from the north like fog. This was the result of dust storms in the Sahara that raised fine dirt 30,000 feet in the air and wafted it southward. There were times when it was so dense that visibility was reduced to a few hundred feet. By the time it reached us, it was not a windstorm—just a gentle blanket of dust on everything.

That was dry season in Gadaka.

When the rains arrived, it was a great moment of celebration. The air was instantly scrubbed clean. The dirt that covered everything was washed back down to the ground. Green again burst out in the grass and trees.

This event signaled something else. It was time to stop all other activity and begin farming. No one knew how long the rains would last that season, so it was critical after the first rainfall to head to the farm and start planting. Nothing else was important at that moment.

The coming of the first rains illustrates a simple principle of time management. There are two Greek words for time. **Chronos** is the word that refers to minutes, hours, and days. It is the normal word we use for time. **Kairos** is something different. It carries the idea of capitalizing on an opportunity.

Time management in Western cultures tends to focus on *chronos*. They are concerned with how to put more minutes in the day—or at least do more in the minutes available. While that may be important, good time management is concerned with both *chronos* and *kairos*.

Kairos is illustrated in the planting season. There was a short window of time to get the seeds in the ground. The growing season was short. If the villagers didn't plant right after the first rains, there might not be enough time for the crops to mature before the rains stopped. That critical time slot is called *kairos*.

The Bible states that God is in control of both kinds of time. *It is not for you to know the times [CHRONOS], or seasons [KAIROS] that the Father has fixed by his own authority* (Acts 1:7).

The villagers were also concerned with both kinds of time. Their survival depended on it.

KAIROS

This word for time refers to opportunity. *Kairos* is quality of time as contrasted with the quantity implied in *chronos*. The villagers applied *kairos* primarily to the planting season. But this has much larger application.

Businessmen understand timing the markets. There are seasons when expanding their business is good and other times when it is best to hold back. *Kairos* is that golden opportunity in the business cycle to increase profits.

There is a story in the Bible about anti-Semitism. The entire nation of Israel was threatened with extermination. Esther happened to be in the right place at the right time. She had access to the king to plead the case for the preservation of her countrymen. Her cousin Mordecai encouraged her to be bold. He framed the context of her situation by pointing out that perhaps she was in this position *for such a time as this* (Esther 4:14). That was *kairos*. She had that golden opportunity that would never present itself again. She could either take advantage of it or lose it forever.

Time management is more than just managing the minutes in an hour. It includes understanding and acting in the context in which we live and operate. It is seeing and taking advantage of open doors that may shut again tomorrow. It is stepping through doors of opportunity while they are still open. *Kairos* means you strike while the iron is hot. It is the spirit of *carpe diem*.

Acting on *kairos* moments means setting aside other priorities. It means that something on the schedule is going to get nudged aside or eliminated. The villagers understood that the day after the first rain was the time to be in their farms. Other odd jobs had to wait. Building fences or erecting their next mud hut would be done another day. The wise farmer wasted no time taking advantage of the moist soil.

The *chronos*-oriented people in Western culture often miss opportunities because they don't appear in a Day-Timer or digital scheduler. There is no way to plan for *kairos*. It is possible to be so tied to appointments and schedules that opportunity blows right past, and we hardly feel the breeze.

It takes wisdom to know when to act. History is full of examples of missed *kairos* moments:

Thomas Edison invented the phonograph but said to his assistant, "This is of no commercial value."[14]

Thomas Watson (chairman of IBM in 1943): "I think there is a world market for about five computers."[15]

Ken Olsen (president of Digital Equipment Corporation, 1977): "There is no reason for any individual to have a computer in their home."[16]

Robert Millikan (Nobel Prize-winning physicist, 1920): "There is no likelihood that man can ever tap the power of the atom."[17]

We may smile at these statements now. We would have probably agreed with them at that time. All of us can remember missed opportunities. There were times when we should have bought a specific stock, should have affirmed a loved one now dead, should have purchased a home (or sold one), should have taken a new job, should have accepted a dinner invitation. . . .

So the question that should grab our attention is: What *kairos* am I missing right now? What seems radical at the moment but will be sensible a decade from now?

Joachim Prinsloo was a farmer in South Africa the end of the 19th Century. Prinsloo was one of those sit-on-the-front-porch-with-a-shotgun kind of guys. Good fortune kept pestering him, but he refused to take advantage of it. He owned a farm that just happened to be on the main reef of gold running east to west just outside the city of Johannesburg. Prospectors kept agitating him until he sold. He unknowingly gave up mineral rights to one of the world's richest gold mines.

Prinsloo moved farther north and bought another farm. It wasn't long before prospectors showed up on his new farm, but this time they were searching for diamonds. This time he wouldn't budge. It was only after his death that the prospectors bought the farm from his daughter.

Here is the rest of the story. A diamond pipe was discovered on this property that became one of the richest mines in the world. It is the only mine where blue diamonds are found. It also produced the Cullinan diamond that is the largest diamond ever discovered. This stone was 3,106 carats as a rough gem. It was cut into many smaller stones, the largest of them ending up in the crown jewels in England. There is no way to place a value on this one stone, much less the thousands of other diamonds from this mine. Now, 100 years later, diamonds are still being surfaced from this mine.

Prinsloo missed his *kairos*—twice! He could have had gold and diamonds but ended up with maize and cattle. Obviously, farming was important to him, and maybe that is all that really matters. Wealth may have destroyed him.

That illustrates the other side of *kairos*. It is not always wise to take advantage of every opportunity that comes our way. There is a time to say no. That is the difficult thing about *kairos*. Is this a really good opportunity or merely a distraction? Is this an open door or merely a side entrance that leads to a dead-end alley?

Sometimes *kairos* moments appear to be interruptions. For those of us who are project-oriented, we hate them. Our schedules are already established. We have deadlines. The next meeting is about to start. Then someone intrudes into our day without an appointment. That raises the big question: Is this *kairos* or a waste of time? Stewardship of time demands an answer to that question.

There is no clinical, scientific way to answer that question. But there is a grid through which you can process your response.

1. Does this *kairos* fulfill your mission, vision, and values in life? It may be a great opportunity, but if it diverts from your purpose for life, it is probably not for you. It doesn't matter how many diamonds are available if it doesn't fit who you are. Digging the mine of this *kairos* is for someone else.

2. Does this *kairos* serve others in a positive way? The most important agenda on earth is not our projects—it is people. Ten years from now it will not matter that we missed a deadline, but our attention to others may change a life.

CHRONOS

The other side of the time management coin is *chronos*. This is the way we utilize the minutes and hours of our day. It is linear time. It is the stuff that weeks, months, and years are made of. It is our schedules, appointments, and watches. This was not an issue in our village in Africa. No one had clocks. At best, they timed things by the position of the sun in the sky. Even so, the village in Africa illustrated a classic picture of this kind of time management.

Africans have an incredible ability to balance loads on their heads. It was common to see people walking down the road with a large bundle of firewood or a clay pot of water from the well. A "donut" made of grass became the buffer for the load so that their hands were free. They balanced huge burdens and walked as casually as if nothing were on their heads.

They hauled building supplies on their heads unless they were wealthy enough to own a donkey. A basket full of rocks and sand was lifted with the help of another onto the head and walked back to the building site. For the sake of efficiency, it was good to carry both rocks and sand at the same time.

Here is the simple genius of the process that translates into a fundamental time management principle. They put the rocks in the basket first—and then the sand. That sounds logical. If the sand went in first, it would be difficult to add rocks. But if the rocks went in first, the sand filtered down between the rocks.

The simple principle is merely this: Put the big stuff in first—then the small stuff. That is the key to *chronos* time management. Put the big stuff in the schedule first, then let the less important stuff fill in the cracks.

That means we have to know what the "big stuff" is. The tendency is to let the urgent items dominate or to let the routine, mundane work push the major projects out of the way. Email, phone calls, filing, sorting, casual conversations, and less important projects wedge their way into our day. Good time management means we will first prioritize what is most important to accomplish and then let everything else filter into the time cracks of our day. Get the big rocks in first. They are normally our key performance areas.

Parkinson's Law suggests that the time spent on any matter is usually inversely proportional to its importance. The Pareto Principle states the same thing another way: that 80 percent of the results come from 20 percent of the effort. There are a few really important things we do that matter. Good time management demands that we know which effort is most important.

Project-oriented people tend to be really good at *chronos*. People-oriented people tend to be good at *kairos*. But leaders don't have the luxury of being unbalanced. They must do both.

Most of life is made up of *chronos*. *Kairos* opportunities come along only once in a while. But if a leader is disciplined in the use of *chronos*, he will be able to take advantage of the *kairos*. The person who is constantly mismanaging the hours of the day cannot stop to capitalize on the *kairos*. If he has control of *chronos*, he has a better chance of taking advantage of a *kairos* moment.

Therefore the starting place is to be diligent in setting priorities and monitoring a schedule. We don't have control over *kairos*. Those normally appear unexpectedly. We do have control over *chronos,* so the key to good time management is to plan our day but be flexible enough to bend when opportunity knocks.

Scripture urges us to place a high value on *chronos.* Psalm 90:12 says: *So teach us to number our days that we may get a heart of wisdom.* The word *number* is a mathematical term that means to account for something. It means to assign value. The Psalmist urges us to view *chronos* as a valuable asset. Imagine that you are paid $10,000 an hour. Many of us use our hours as if we are getting paid minimum wage. The Bible says to assign an enormous value to the hours of the day. What difference would it make in your schedule if you did indeed get paid $10,000 an hour? The rest of the verse answers that question: you will *get a heart of wisdom.* You will use your time much more wisely by assigning a high value.

Operating by both *chronos* and *kairos* will help a leader in many ways.

- He will stop managing by crisis.

- He will begin planning his day.

- He will stop attempting to accomplish too much.

- He will effectively delegate or delete tasks.

- He will evaluate telephone "interruptions" and drop-in visitors.

- He will stop procrastinating.

- He will increase his ability to say no.

- He will eliminate some of the inconsequential activities of his schedule.

- He will be able to capitalize on those once-in-a-lifetime opportunities.

- He will ultimately align with Psalm 90:12.

In summary, you don't need a stopwatch to manage time well. The villagers of Gadaka never had a timepiece. They did, however, understand time management better than many of us in the digital age surrounded by timepieces.

8

HORNBILLS

Servant leadership

*You know that those who are considered rulers
of the Gentiles lord it over them, and their great ones
exercise authority over them. But it shall not be so
among you. But whoever would be great among you
must be your servant.*
Mark 10: 42-43

*Do not forget what it is to be a sailor
because of being a captain yourself.*
Tanzanian proverb

African birds are incredible. They vary in size from a three-inch hummingbird to the eight-foot ostrich. They range from the extreme beauty of the peacock to outright repulsive carrion-eating buzzards. African birds are noisy—not the tweet-tweet of a dainty canary, but ruckus-irritating squawking and screeching. There are more than 2000 species of birds on the continent.

Hornbills (bucerotidae) are common in Africa. They vary in size up to fifteen inches tall with a brightly colored, long, down-curved bill. Strong neck muscles support their oversized beaks with the first two vertebrae fused together to carry the weight. This bill is practical for fighting, constructing a nest, preening, and catching prey. There are twenty-three different varieties of the hornbill in sub-Saharan Africa.

These birds form monogamous pairs for life. It is this relationship that gives a powerful object lesson of servant leadership. Here is how it works.

The female lays up to six white eggs in a nest created in a hollow tree. Five days before laying eggs she climbs into the crevice and, with the help of her mate, begins sealing up the entrance. Mud, droppings, and fruit pulp are the building material. They close the entrance until there is only a small hole left. This construction project can be done in just a few hours; at most it takes a few days. The practical side of this strategy is that it protects the mother and the eggs from predators.

For twenty-five days, the mother sits on the eggs to incubate them. But the obvious dilemma is that she cannot get out to eat. This is where servant leadership appears. Her mate spends his day foraging for food and bringing it to her, passing it through the narrow opening. They eat seeds, small insects, spiders, scorpions, termites, and ants. Without his service, she would die. For that month of incubation, he lives life for her benefit.

This is the essence of servant leadership. It is the opposite of dictatorial leadership. It is the spirit of serving those you lead rather than being served. It is being more concerned about the success of followers than self-advancement. It is looking out for the cares and concerns of others above self-interests.

Robert K. Greenleaf (1904-1990) is frequently credited for coining the term "servant leadership." He may have popularized the approach, but this existed long before Greenleaf started writing. It goes back at least 2000 years to the consummate leader, Jesus.

Jesus brought about a radical paradigm shift in leadership. In those days, being king meant you were in charge and could demand servitude from others. Jesus came along and turned that model on its head. Instead of climbing a corporate ladder to bark orders at those below, Jesus stooped low to support those above. It is called servant leadership. Jesus put it this way:

> You know that the rulers of the Gentiles lord it over them, and their great ones exercise authority over them. It shall not be so among you. But whoever would be great among you must be your servant, and whoever would be first among you must be your slave, even as the Son of Man came not to be served but to serve, and to give his life as a ransom for many (Matthew 20:25-28).

Verse 26 talks about being "great" if you are a servant. Verse 27 speaks of being "first" if you are a slave. There is a difference between a servant and a slave. A big difference. One is an employee; the other is merely property. It would probably be more appropriate to call this "slave leadership" rather than "servant leadership."

This mini sermon came right after a mother approached Jesus asking a favor to have her sons sit on the throne with Him. It seems the sons put her up to this. The rest of the disciples were incensed at their bravado and selfishness. Maybe they were most upset because these two thought of it first.

In His answer to this request, Jesus completely shifted the model of leadership. It wasn't merely words. He immediately demonstrated the idea for them with a blind man sitting beside the road. Jesus asked, *What do you want me to do for you?* (Matthew 20:32). It is amazing that the leader of the universe sought to serve instead of be served.

The prevailing model of His day was "What can you do for me?" Jesus said just the opposite: *What can I do for you?* In another setting, Jesus showed the way by washing His disciples' feet.

To drive this truth home He said, *For who is the greater, one who reclines at table or one who serves? Is it not the one who reclines at table? But I am among you as the one who serves* (Luke 22:27).

Jesus also said,

> *You know that those who are considered rulers of the Gentiles lord it over them, and their great ones exercise authority over them. But it shall not be so among you. But whoever would be great among you must be your servant* (Mark 10: 42-43).

The leadership style of the village chief in our Nigerian village was "command and control." He obviously had not taken lessons from the hornbill. His word was law. He told villagers which plot of land they could farm. He settled disputes and was final court of law. His word was final.

Top-down leadership is the opposite of servant leadership. An autocratic leader has an agenda that is focused solely on his personal desires. The key word there is *solely*. A leader obviously must have an agenda, a vision, and a strategy. But there is a different spirit in the person who is a servant leader. He doesn't use people to accomplish the vision. He uses the vision to advance people and causes.

Autocratic leadership works. It is effective. It gets things done. It is successful if success is measured only by the bottom line. It is intimidating and coerces compliance, but that doesn't make it right.

Forcing others damages relationships. Appendix B at the end of this book shows a sliding scale between autocratic and servant leadership. Dictatorship is the antithesis of leadership. It is a lack of leadership. It occurs when people are not following. That is why they must be forced. It is driving from behind instead of leading from up front.

Remember the definition for leadership used in this book: *A leader is a godly servant who knows where he is going and inspires and equips others to follow.* The word *servant* is very deliberately placed in that sentence. This is not a word to fill space or sound good. It is the essence of a philosophy of leadership. The preponderance of focus on the topic of leadership in the Bible leans toward being a servant. The term *leader* only appears six times in the Bible. The term *servant* appears more than 900 times.

Biblical Ministries Worldwide helps local churches send missionaries to the field. Non-denominational churches utilize the services of this mission agency to help screen, train, mobilize, and support their missionaries. Each year we conduct two candidate orientations to accept new missionaries into the organization. I routinely tell candidates that if they join BMW, they are not coming to work for me. Rather, I will work for them. It is my role to provide support systems so that they can succeed in their vision and calling. They are not accomplishing my agenda. I am most concerned in their fulfillment of God's agenda.

I was a missionary in Africa for seventeen years. When I moved to the U.S.A. to become the director of this organization, someone congratulated me on my promotion. I was quick to adjust his understanding. This was not a promotion but rather a demotion. It was not a step upwards, it was a step downwards. As a missionary, there were leaders serving me. Now I had the responsibility of serving others. This was not a move up a corporate ladder. Now I stood at the bottom of the ladder supporting those above me.

Part of my responsibility is to provide accountability for those in the mission family. I could never do that except for the fact that I am under authority. It is healthy to have someone looking over my shoulder. I gladly report to a board of directors and value their watch care over my life and ministry. It helps me to stay focused and do the right things. Then as I provide supervision for others, it is with the attitude of how can I help them succeed in their ministry. My aim is not to find someone doing something wrong. My role is to encourage colleagues in the right direction. My input is aimed at helping them to excel.

When we moved from Africa to the States, everything was new to us. We sought a church to attend and visited many in an attempt to find a place where we could minister. There is one thing that tipped the scales for us. Lebanon

Baptist Church has a rather large property with a lot of parking spaces. Some of those slots were really near the building. But I noticed that when we would pull into the parking lot on a Sunday morning, the pastor's car was parked the farthest from the worship center. By all rights, it would seem the pastor would have a dedicated spot with a sign chasing everyone else away. After all, he was the pastor. The fact that Pastor Hester would walk farther than anyone else immediately signaled the heart of a servant leader. That clinched our decision.

Humility is the primary character trait of a servant leader. John MacArthur writes the following in his book *A Few Good Shepherds:*

> God's plan for leadership is ministry not management, not governing monarchs, but humble slaves, not slick celebrities, but laboring servants. Those who lead God's people must above all exemplify sacrifice, devotion, submission and lowliness. Jesus was the pattern when He stooped to wash feet. In light of that no leader has the right to think of himself as a bigwig. Spiritual leadership requires a godly, gifted, multi-skilled man of integrity who must maintain a humble perspective and demeanor. No flock will survive and prosper if its shepherd (leader) tries to trade his staff for a throne.[18]

The Bible makes a big deal about humility. It puts it this way:

> *God opposes the proud, but gives grace to the humble* (James 4:6).

Humble yourselves before the Lord, and he will exalt you (James 4:10).

God opposes the proud, but gives grace to the humble (1 Peter 5:5).

Put on then, as God's chosen ones, holy and beloved, compassionate hearts, kindness, humility, meekness, and patience (Colossians 3:12).

Very closely aligned with humility is the topic of brokenness. This is rarely discussed as a qualification for leadership, but it is foundational in Christian leadership. Brokenness leads to humility. A common path for men in ministry is to graduate from a Bible college or seminary. The temptation is to head into ministry with all the answers. There is an idealistic vision of how things will be. The first few years of ministry tend to realign those expectations. Ministry is not as easy as it seemed in the classroom. Expectations are lowered. Hopes and aspirations are a little more reasonable.

But a quantum leap is taken when someone is "broken." There are many delivery vehicles for brokenness. It may come through a major failure. It could happen because of sickness or persecution. It might be through struggles with raising children. But once a person hits the wall and comes to the end of himself, he is now poised for a new dimension of leadership.

Gene Edwards writes about this topic in his book *A Tale of Three Kings.*

> God has a university. It is a small school. Few enroll; even fewer graduate. Very, very few indeed. God has this school because he does not have broken men and women. Instead, he has several other types of people. He has people who claim to have God's authority . . . and don't – people who claim to be broken . . . and aren't. And people who do have God's authority, but who are mad and unbroken. And he has, regretfully, a great mixture of everything in between. All these he has in abundance, but broken men and women, hardly at all.[19]

The broken person has a spirit of tenderness that did not exist before. There is more patience for those who may not reach "the standard." There is sensitivity to the struggles of others. There is an empathy that pervades the mindset of the leader. At a point of brokenness, the leader enters a totally different arena of capacity to lead.

The Bible also speaks to this topic:

> *When the righteous cry for help, the* LORD *hears and delivers them out of all their troubles. The* LORD *is near to the brokenhearted and saves the crushed in spirit* (Psalm 34:17-18).

> *The sacrifices of God are a broken spirit; a broken and contrite heart, O God, you will not despise* (Psalm 51:17).

When Solomon died, his son Rehoboam took over. As a young man he was seeking to establish a philosophy of leadership for himself. He asked his father's advisors and their answer was *If you will be a servant to this people today and serve them . . . then they will be your servants forever* (1 Kings 12:7).

Rehoboam didn't like that advice so he went to his peers and asked their opinion. They said exactly the opposite. In fact they suggested he become heavy-handed and dictatorial to the level of being abusive. He rejected the advice of his father's counselors and became autocratic. The result was that he split the kingdom.

That story has been reenacted thousands of times throughout history. Many a church has been splintered because someone wanted to be the boss. Self-seeking leadership may work for a while. It can even have the appearance of success. But ultimately, there is going to be division and strife.

Corrupt leadership suppresses opposing views. It takes the position of "my way or the highway." The corrupt leader seeks to control everything and make every decision. He is manipulative. He threatens. He gets rid of opposition and those who would question him. His insecurity makes him suspicious of everyone. His raised sword produces conformity. He controls behavior. It is cultic.

This stands in direct contrast to the leadership style of Jesus. He led by relationships. As a shepherd, He knew His sheep. He was interested in the disciples' success. He empowered others to act. He quietly took mistreatment and misunderstanding for the sake of His followers. He wasn't intimidated by dissent or disagreement. He was no pushover but worked with those who had "an ear to hear." He took advantage of failure in others to help them be better.

In his book *Good to Great* Jim Collins studied eleven major corporations to discover what elements made these companies so successful. One of his finds was that most of the time the CEO was "quiet, humble, modest, reserved, shy, mild-mannered, self-effacing, understated."[20] Even the secular world understands the importance of servant leadership.

All this raises the question of whether or not a servant leader can have any vision, goals, opinions, or backbone. If he is serving others, can he personally have an agenda? How does the vision of the church or organization or business fit into this?

A servant is an employee. Since he works for someone else, he is fulfilling the job defined by someone else. He is normally given a mission and vision for fulfilling his job. The time to address these issues is before taking the job. It is unethical to come into a church or organization with a hidden agenda. During the candidate process for a job it is critical to make sure that mission and values are in sync. It is not uncommon that a leader is employed to craft the vision. This means he will own it because he participated in creating it. If the day arrives where the leader veers from the stated mission, values, and vision, he must declare his direction and face the possibility that he may no longer be the one to serve in that capacity.

The chief of our village had never heard about Jesus or Robert Greenleaf. We might give him a pass since he was merely following hundreds of years of tradition without the influence of Scripture. But he did have the hornbill as an example.

9

MUD HUTS

The beauty of simplicity

*And I . . . did not come proclaiming to you
the testimony of God with lofty speech or wisdom.*
1 Corinthians 2:1

You must eat an elephant one bite at a time.
African proverb

A mud hut is about as simple as it gets—a circle of mud walls with a thatched roof. Nothing complex. Simplicity at its best. No scaffolding. No architects. No blueprints. No building inspectors. No corners. No levels. No plumbing or electricity. There is one opening for a door and maybe a hole for a window. A room with a roof. The building materials are free and plentiful. All it takes is some initiative to gather and arrange things.

The rondavel is one of those quintessential icons of Africa. It was standard housing in the village of Gadaka where I grew up. A family might have several huts surrounded by a wall made of thatch or woven mats.

Building a hut is simple. The first step is to mix the mud with grass. No machines needed. Just stomping in mud like the grape vats of Italy. This was heaven for a six-year-old boy in Africa. Where else could playing in mud be called work? The mud was then rolled into oversized sausages and smeared one layer on top of another until the walls reached six feet. No bricks. Just layer on layer of mud. The rondavel was then capped with a simple round hat of thatch attached to a framework of sticks.

Not much to it. Just a functional African hut that has provided shelter and housing for thousands of years. The same idea is replicated around the world. It may be called a yurt (Mongolia), igloo (Canada), teepee (America), hytte

(Norway) or burdei (Ukraine). The idea is still the same. Simplicity.

Science and industry have added complexity to everything. Progress in civilization has complicated life. Occasionally, companies like Apple are able to rise above the morass of complexity. Steve Jobs perfected the art of keeping it simple. In spite of the millions of circuits, wires, and pixels, Apple creates products that have clean lines. They have branded themselves with the concept of simplicity.

One of the keys to effective leadership is the ability to take complexity and distill it down to its bare essence. Complexity confuses followers. Simplicity brings clarity. A leader's role is to bring clarity out of confusion. If something is simple, it is easy to understand.

The good leader does not worry about appearing simple. He revels in it. There is a fine line between making something simple and being ignorant or uneducated. A good leader's ego can handle accusations of being simplistic. He may not appear intellectual, but that is not his goal. Understanding, clarity, and action are his objectives. His goal is to be uncomplicated. Albert Einstein put it this way: "If you can't explain it to a six-year-old, you don't understand it."[21] We could hardly accuse Einstein of being ignorant.

Jesus had the incomparable ability to make things simple. His parables corralled massive ideas into profound lessons that even children could follow. Deep theological issues were compressed into short, pithy proclamations.

One day He was asked to summarize the entire Bible. His answer was simply to love God and love people (Matthew 22:37-39). Doing those two things takes care of all the other expectations of Scripture. Nothing complicated. It is easy to remember. Out of thousands of words and hundreds of commands, He gave us a summary that all of us can comprehend.

The military is exceptional at concise communication. They have to be. They understand that in the heat of battle, there is no time for complicated commands. It is simply "Charge!" or "Retreat!" or "Fire!"

It was the 1972 Easter offensive. Col. John Ripley was leading 600 soldiers on the front lines of the battle. A river separated them from 20,000 North Vietnamese with 200 tanks. The enemy was preparing to cross the one bridge that connected each side. They were grossly outnumbered with no chance of victory.

Ripley radioed his commander with a call for reinforcements. The response was simple: "Hold and die!"

Nothing complex about that order. Ripley knew exactly what was expected. It meant there would be no reinforcements. They were on their own. All they could do was heroically fight until death.

The simplicity and clarity of those orders immediately changed Ripley and his men. He said, "When you know you are going to die, a wonderful thing happens. You stop being cluttered by the feeling you have to save yourself."[22]

Ripley and a few men strapped explosives to their backs and headed toward the river. With the enemy shooting at them they scrambled hand over hand under the bridge. They rigged 500 pounds of dynamite and got back to the safety of their shore before detonating the explosives. The destruction of the bridge held back the opposing forces.

This all happened because of the simplicity and clarity of a commander's communication. Imagine what would have happened if there had been a two-hour conversation about what to do next. Ripley's commander understood the value of concise communication.

There are a number of ways that simplicity will help a leader excel.

Subject Mastery - Leaders are often expected to understand complex issues. They have not really understood until they can state them simply.

A mission statement is a good way to see whether a leader understands the big picture. The purpose statement of an organization or business distills the very simple and important answer as to why it exists.

The most fundamental statement about an organization is their mission statement. A leader cannot lead well until he can articulate it. It is normally one short sentence. It is memorable. It encapsulates everything the organization does. If it is stated and explained simply, he will understand his marching orders.

The best leaders have the ability to connect many disconnected ideas. Nelson Mandela was a master at this. One of the many stories of this capacity was portrayed in the movie *Invictus*.

Mandela had recently taken over the presidency of South Africa. After serving twenty-seven years in prison, he emerged with a statesman's view of politics. He understood that there was no room for retaliation for the years of apartheid. He rose above any thought of retribution. He understood that despite the past record of the whites in South Africa, they were an integral part of society that would benefit the country.

While rugby was a sport of the Europeans who had imprisoned him, he embraced it. He honored the sport that was the heart language of the white population. He leveraged sports to unite a nation.

In spite of the complexity of a nation with a dozen languages, multiple cultures, and a dissonant past, he focused on one simple idea: rugby. Other leaders may have attempted to talk about thousands of laws that needed to be changed. Mandela kept it simple. His public actions centered on uniting the country with a World Cup victory.

He did it. For a brief period in history, the citizens of a divided country rose in a swell of pride and unity that had never been experienced in all its history.

Another example of this principle is personified in Bruce Wilkinson. During his seminary days he wondered if it would be possible to teach the entire Old Testament of the Bible in one day. Could a person learn every major event, person, and place within a few hours? The answer to that question produced the organization called Walk Thru the Bible.

This is a classic example of taking massive amounts of data and distilling them to a manageable size. It demonstrates Wilkinson's personal mastery of the material. It is easy to get lost in the details of the Old Testament. Hundreds of stories seem to stand alone without any interconnectedness. With Walk Thru, a person can immediately connect with the context of any portion of the Old Testament.

Vision - A second application of simplicity is found in the vision statement of an organization. Casting vision is one of the primary roles of a leader. Planning for the future is foundational to the job description of those who lead. Whoever points to the next destination and gets people to follow is the leader.

The good leader must be able to state his vision simply. The shorter the statement the better. It is not unusual to take twelve to twenty-four months to come up with the vision of an organization. There are normally hundreds of issues that converge. Thousands of details pour into the pot. Ultimately, out of the visioneering exercise a short, pithy statement must come that clearly defines the desired future of the organization.

Here are some examples:

> The vision statement of Jesus was simply **to take the gospel to every person in every place.**

> The vision statement of some local churches is simply **to make more and better disciples.**

> The vision statement of Calvary Community Church in Westlake Village, California, is **"Love God more, love people more, love more people."**

> The current vision statement for Biblical Ministries Worldwide is to be an organization **advancing and empowered by prayer.** That is the one drum we beat. While there are hundreds of issues we constantly address, prayer is the one big idea.

> The previous vision statement for Biblical Ministries Worldwide was **500/500/500.** That meant we wanted to establish a special relationship with 500 sending churches, grow to a mission family of 500 missionaries, and start 500 new churches around the world.

> As leader of this mission agency, I have distilled my job description down to this short phrase: **to articulate and activate the vision.** Everything I do flows from that simple statement.

> Microsoft is reported to have set a goal over 30 years ago **to put a computer on every desk.**

> Nike's current vision is **to be the number one athletic company in the world.**

Southwest Airlines: **to make air travel cheaper and more convenient than auto travel.**

Wal-Mart: **worldwide leader in retail.**

The common denominator in all of these statements is simplicity. Everyone in the organization or company can grasp and remember the big idea.

An "elevator speech" is the ability to state simply the overall mission, vision, and values of an organization between the ground floor and the tenth floor. A good leader will be able to do that. If he can't do it, then things are too complex. Ultimately, the vision of an organization must be simple.

Communication - A third application of simplicity in leadership is the ability to speak in a way that everyone understands. It is the old adage, "The burden of communication is on the communicator." It is the leader's responsibility to make sure people understand. Therefore, the effective leader speaks with simplicity and clarity. He doesn't blame others for not understanding. Arthur Schopenhauer, a 19th Century German philosopher, put it this way: "One should use common words to say uncommon things."[23]

This principle shows up in a variety of ways. The art of delegation is a foundational leadership skill. It is not enough to know what to delegate. The effective leader knows how to delegate. Instructions must be communicated in such a way that the follower knows exactly what the leader wants. The leader cannot really be upset with outcomes if he has not delegated with clarity and simplicity.

This concept is most evident in speeches and sermons. The highly educated academic may revel in confusing listeners or feel a sense of superiority because he speaks above their heads. The effective leader is looking for results. In that case there cannot be any confusion. The leader's role is not to impress others with vocabulary. His goal is for everyone to understand.

It is easier to speak for one hour than it is to speak for seven minutes. A communicator should not speak for an hour unless he can say it in seven minutes. The condensed version indicates that the speaker understands the core of his message. Sometimes you can say more by saying less.

At one time I taught homiletics (the science and art of preaching) to future pastors. While preaching appears to be an easy task to the person in the pew, it is a very complex process. To simplify the task, I distilled the entire process down to seven steps. This allowed the apprentice to progressively move through each phase until a sermon emerged.

1. Do a word study.
2. Outline the passage.
3. Compare other passages.

4. Consult commentaries.

5. Create an outline.

6. Add illustrations and application.

7. Add introduction and conclusion.

Communication is a major part of any leader's job. His capacity to connect with the minds and hearts of followers will often determine his success. Leaders like Abraham Lincoln, Martin Luther King, and Ronald Reagan had one thing in common: they knew how to communicate with simplicity. We still talk about the Gettysburg Address primarily because it captured major themes and took less than a minute to deliver. Most can recall portions of the "I have a dream" speech because it distilled King's vision into pithy, piercing statements. We understand Reagan's vision through his simple imagery of a shining city on a hill. Who can forget "Tear down this wall!" which summarized his over-all vision of ending the Cold War? Communication and simplicity are mandatory for good leadership.

Communicating simply is often difficult, but it is the mark of a good leader. Another leadership lesson I learned in the village in Africa is the illustration of the simplicity of a mud hut. The next time you are called upon to lead, KEEP IT SIMPLE.

10

THE BLACKSMITH

The value of mentoring and apprenticeships

Just as you learned it from Epaphras . . . .
Colossians 1:7

Leadership is best taught by a leader.
Ugandan proverb

The blacksmith's workshop was one of my favorite places in the village to visit. It wasn't really a "shop." A thatched roof without walls formed the workspace. This was a fascinating place for a kid.

The blacksmith had the simple tools of a hammer and an anvil. Well, the anvil wasn't the real thing—it was just a chunk of metal. Sitting cross-legged on the ground, the blacksmith would hammer pieces of metal into a hoe or machete. It was noisy, hot, and exciting. The sparks would fly giving us the closest thing to a fireworks display that could be found in an African village.

The metal was heated red-hot in a fire pit. This was the job of the blacksmith's apprentice. It was ingenious in its simplicity. The leather from the hind legs of a goat formed the bellows. The narrow end (by the hoof) was attached to a metal tube that forced the air to a single point in the middle of the charcoal.

The apprentice had a way of opening and closing the large end of the leather billows as he pumped. Spreading his fingers in a backward motion opened the skin to draw in air. Then he clamped the skin bag closed as he pressed the bellows down to expel the air through the narrow tube. It was a continuous motion. As the left hand pulled back to draw in air, the right hand would pump air into the fire. Soon the fire was blazing and the apprentice was exhausted.

There were no colleges or trade schools available to learn how to be a blacksmith. Remember, this was a remote village in Africa. But generation after generation of blacksmiths had furnished this village with metal implements.

The process of training the next blacksmith is so simple that we have largely set it aside. Western education has replaced training with talking. The experienced blacksmith trained someone younger to take over. Each blacksmith had a trainee who pumped the bellows and learned the trade by watching and helping the master craftsman. Nothing sophisticated. No classroom. No exams. No chalkboard or PowerPoint presentations. But in the end, a master craftsman emerged.

Apprenticeships have been the primary educational tool in most of world history. It has been a time-tested approach to training the next generation in most trades and careers. Western education has tended to veer away from this teaching technique. There is, however, great potential and value in the blacksmith's approach.

From the heat of the blacksmith shop emerge some basic leadership principles. There is nothing new here; it is just that we don't really do this much anymore. The village blacksmith suggests three basic lessons.

1. THE VALUE OF TRAINING LEADERS

One of the core competencies of a good leader is the ability to delegate. An effective leader understands he must focus on the few things that only he can do. Everything else is handed off for someone else to accomplish. There is one thing, however, that no leader can delegate: training others. No one but the village blacksmith could train blacksmiths. No one but the leader can train leaders. Followers will not train leaders. Leaders must train leaders.

The first line of any leader's job description could be the same. It doesn't matter what his job title may be. If someone is a leader, he should train leaders.

Jack Welch was the CEO of General Electric but devoted 30 percent of his workweek to training leaders. If the leader of the world's largest corporation committed that amount of time, it must be important. The village blacksmith needed someone to man the bellows, but there was a higher purpose in having an apprentice. The future of the village was at stake. He had to train someone or the craft would die.

There is a price to pay if a leader is going to train leaders. There may be several reasons leaders do not commit to mentoring leaders:

They are possessive. These leaders like to hold on to their jobs. They fear someone else may take over. If they train someone else, that person may end up a better blacksmith and steal their customers. Most leaders love their job. They are not about to give it away.

They lack patience. It is faster and easier to do it yourself. It takes time to train others and watch them stumble and fumble. Many leaders just don't have the patience to let others try.

They are perfectionists. The danger of handing the hammer to the apprentice is that the hoe will not turn out well. Quality of products from the blacksmith's shop will go down. It will take time to correct the imperfections. Customers will not be happy with inferior products. It costs money to go back and re-do the mistakes of the apprentice, so it is easier for the perfectionist just to do it himself.

They love privacy. Training an apprentice means you have a shadow. It requires opening the door to your private space. It is not always comfortable to have someone looking over your shoulder, so instead of inviting an intruder into his workspace, the leader just doesn't train others.

There is no question about it—it takes commitment on the part of the leader to train leaders. Part of the entertainment in the blacksmith shop was to hear the blacksmith ranting and raving against the apprentice. But in spite of the incompetence of the apprentice, the blacksmith knew he needed him. So he committed to training.

This begs the question: Are leaders born or trained? There are definitely born leaders. Some seem to demonstrate that while still in diapers. There are a small handful of individuals who just innately seem to know how to lead.

These take-charge people suck all the oxygen out of the room by their mere presence. They just know what to do.

But . . . the majority of leaders have had to learn how to lead.

The reason this is possible is that much of leadership involves things that are transferable. The building blocks of leadership involve character, skills, and knowledge. All of those things can be learned.

Character - Trustworthiness, dependability, diligence, self-discipline, tenacity, and honesty are all character traits that enable a person to lead. Obviously there are those who are corrupt and still lead, but it is a corrupt leadership. The irony is that the most corrupt leader still wants people around him who have character, people he can trust.

Skills - Delegation, strategizing, managing, writing, conflict resolution, teamwork, visioneering, people skills, communication, and time management are all skills that are needed to lead. It is possible to coach and apprentice in each of these disciplines.

Knowledge - Facts about the product, business principles, accounting, decision-making, and financial management are academic issues that can be learned in a classroom. Western education is most comfortable with this one since most of us graduated from a knowledge-based philosophy of education.

The point is that leadership can be learned. The only question is whether or not present-day leaders will commit to passing this on to the next generation of leaders.

2. THE VALUE OF NON-FORMAL EDUCATION

The second basic lesson from the blacksmith shop was the value of non-formal education. This is in contrast to informal and formal education.

Informal education is what happens to children. They touch a stove and learn not to do that again. No one planned the curriculum or had a class on not touching stoves. It just happened. Much of what we have learned in life has happened informally.

On the other end of the continuum is formal education. Those of us in the West were taught this way. It includes classrooms, whiteboards, lectures, fifty-minute sessions, curriculum, accreditation, and exams.

In between those two is non-formal education. It is deliberate. There are specific goals. It is definitely education. It just doesn't take place in a classroom in a sequential curriculum. Think of the apprentice in a blacksmith shop. There were specific knowledge, skills, and character issues to be learned, but they were taught in real time in real life in real work. The blacksmith did not have a classroom with a media projector, handouts, and tests. He simply brought the apprentice into the shop and began working.

The fascinating fact is that Jesus chose to train His key leaders through non-formal education. He lived during a time in which formal education was alive and doing very well. He could have started a school. Instead, He asked some men to walk with Him as He fulfilled His calling in life. He chose 12 men and worked side by side with them for 3½ years.

There was definitely a plan for apprenticing these men. While the curriculum was not written in academic terms or fifty-minute teaching sessions, there was an overall plan for the training. He sent them on meaningful work assignments. They then returned to give feedback and admit to their failures. They were highly motivated to learn when they felt the sting of their inadequacies.

Non-formal education is concerned with doing—not just knowing. Western education focuses primarily on knowing. It is possible to graduate from college with a 4.0 average but still not know how to do the very work for which a student was trained. It is the difference between wisdom and knowledge. It is the difference between passing an exam about blacksmithing and actually hammering out a hoe. Non-formal education is all about doing.

Formal education = Knowledge

Non-Formal education = Knowledge + Skills

This is not to suggest that academics are unimportant. There must be head knowledge. The key lies in the goal of education. Knowledge is not an end in itself. There is no real benefit in just knowing, if you cannot do something with the knowledge. Securing a formal degree and working your way up to Ph.D. does not guarantee you can make a living. Ultimately you must do something with that knowledge.

With Western education it is possible to be credentialed because you have passed enough exams. Non-formal education demands that you can actually do something with the knowledge you have acquired. Graduation in the blacksmith shop takes place when you can hammer a piece of iron into a hoe.

Another major difference between these two models is how you learn. In formal education people learn by listening. In non-formal education the student learns by doing. Instead of a lecture, the non-formal apprenticeship combines teaching with real-life experience. Formal education is classroom-oriented while non-formal education takes place in the workshop of real life.

An additional critical difference between these two models of training is that education takes place *in* work rather than *for* work. Typically, students go to college because someday they will need to get a job and earn a living.

That is formal education. But non-formal education takes place while the student is earning a living. The African apprentice in the blacksmith shop got paid (albeit very little) while he was learning. He was actually pumping the bellows and contributing to the success of the business. He learned in real life circumstances. Experiential training produces something of value, right now.

Accredited degrees have tremendous value. They establish standards for academia. We all benefit from those who focus on systematic learning, writing, and lecturing. We need the institutions of higher learning. But we should not be held captive to university degrees. Our devotion to higher learning may diminish the importance of non-formal education.

In the West we have tended to disregard the value of any learning exercise if there is no credit attached to it. The bird of industry flies with two wings—one is academic and the other is skill. The second wing is just as important as the first wing, for with only one the bird will end up flying in circles. Since formal education focuses very little on skills development, that kind of learning must take place somewhere else. That "somewhere else" could be an apprenticeship. Though there is no degree associated with the apprenticeship, it is just as important (possibly more) as the classroom credit.

3. THE VALUE OF A MENTOR

The blacksmith would never have used the word. *Mentor* would have been a foreign term to him, but the concept of mentoring was not. That is what he did with his apprentice. Long before our contemporary books on the topic, it was happening in a village in Africa.

Being a mentor simply means taking someone under your wing to develop that individual. It encompasses all areas of life. The blacksmith not only trained his apprentice in metal work, he developed him as an individual. He taught him a work ethic. He coached him in people skills and business practice. The apprentice became a much better person because an older person was looking out for him.

Mentoring began, however, long before the blacksmith in Gadaka started the process. The Bible is full of mentoring stories:

Jethro mentored Moses.

Moses mentored Joshua and the elders of Israel.

Joshua mentored the other military leaders.

Deborah mentored Barak.

Eli mentored Samuel.

Samuel mentored Saul and David.

David mentored Solomon.

Elijah mentored Elisha.

Elisha mentored King Jehoash.

Daniel mentored Nebuchadnezzar.

Mordecai mentored Esther.

Jesus mentored the twelve disciples.

The twelve mentored hundreds of other leaders.

Paul mentored Titus, Timothy, and many others.

Timothy mentored "faithful men" such as Epaphras.

Priscilla and **Aquila** mentored Apollos.

There is a distinction between *mentor* and *coach*. Mentor refers to the person's entire being. Coaching applies to acquisition of a specific skill.

We most frequently use *coach* in a sports setting. This is an individual who helps the athlete do much better. He develops the skill of the player. The coach works on one facet of life while the mentor considers the whole. The blacksmith did both.

There is an added dimension to the blacksmith's coaching: he was player/coach. He didn't sit on the sidelines and tell the apprentice how to smith iron—he actually did it. Then he watched as the apprentice tried his hand at it. Instant feedback. Constant critique. The strongest kind of coaching is when the coach gets on the field and demonstrates. That is why leaders need to train leaders. They are already in the game and can demonstrate what they are teaching.

The first step in training someone is first of all to paint a clear picture of what that person needs to do. This takes time and forethought. The mentor's rule is this: START WITH THE END IN MIND. The function, work, skill, or ability must be clear in the mind of the mentor before he can create a training strategy. The blacksmith knew exactly what blacksmiths do; therefore, he could train blacksmiths.

Children are naturally curious and will learn about anything that comes into their world, but adults are different. They tend to learn best when they need to know something. For instance, a father buys his son a toy for Christmas, but it needs to be put together before the kid can play with it. Even though the toy was bought a month before Christmas, dad waits until Christmas morning to read the directions (and even then may not read them). Few men learn how to put the toy together before they need to put the toy together.

Likewise, the coach trains when a specific skill is needed. Vision drives learning. Once the goal of making a hoe is in sight, then the blacksmith knows how to train the apprentice. Appendix A is an example of an outcomes matrix that is used to paint the picture of a church leader. This instrument was created by church-planting missionaries in South Africa. It is a clear picture of what a leader needs to know, be, and do. It starts with the end in mind and then builds a curriculum to get an individual to that point.

A critical decision in this process is choosing the right apprentice. The leader cannot possibly train everyone; he must be selective. But it is difficult to identify the raw material. How do you know who is worth your investment of time? It is a subjective judgment call. There is a level of intuitive sense about choosing the right apprentice, but it is still subjective since no one can forecast the future with complete accuracy.

The Bible takes some of the subjectivity out of the equation, however, and suggests one major test. The one character trait above all else should be faithfulness. Scripture teaches that the primary qualification of an employee needs to be trustworthiness. *Moreover it is required of stewards that they be found faithful* (1 Corinthians 4:2). It is better to train one person who is faithful than one hundred who are not. The one faithful person will do something with his training. The one hundred may do little.

The next logical question is: How do you know if someone is faithful? Jesus gives us the answer to that in Luke 16. There are three ways to observe faithfulness in individuals:

1. Are they faithful in little things (v. 10)? You don't make someone president of the company if he has never shown up for work on time to sweep the floors.

2. Are they faithful in the use of money (v. 11)? Are they in debt? Do they pay their bills on time? Are they in financial bondage?

3. Are they faithful with other people's property (v. 12)? Do they treat company property as their own? Do they steal company time or property?

These are objective measures of a person's faithfulness. The mentor can observe these traits. They become the standard for accepting an apprentice.

An owner of a fast food franchise is reported to have thrown trash in the parking lot as a method of screening potential employees. This vetting process was based on Jesus' method of observing faithfulness: how do they handle other people's property? This boss realized that if a job applicant cared enough to pick up trash in a parking lot that did not belong to him, he might be a good worker. Failure to pick up the paper meant immediate disqualification.

In summary: *leaders produce leaders.* Ralph Nader puts it this way: "I start with the premise that the function of leadership is to produce more leaders, not more followers."[24] In spite of our sophistication in education, we would do well to return to the blacksmith's shop in Nigeria.

11

SAWUBONA

People skills

*Let your speech always be gracious, seasoned with salt,
so that you may know how you ought to
answer each person.*
Colossians 4:6

If your mouth turns into a knife, it will cut off your lips.
African proverb

Most Western greetings are mundane and meaningless. "How are you?" is the standard icebreaker. That inquiry is normally answered by an equally empty "I'm fine." The greeter normally doesn't really care how you are doing and the responder normally isn't all that "fine." This perfunctory greeting moves everyone to further conversation. So we continue to do it.

Greetings in Africa are totally different. The normal Zulu greeting is **Sawubona** (sah-wu-bo-nah). It literally means "I see you." It acknowledges the presence and the importance of the other person. It is a kind and gracious way to acknowledge the worth of an individual. It means my life stops to focus on yours.

Frederick Collins put it this way: "There are two types of people—those who come into a room and say, 'Well, here I am!' and those who come in and say, 'Ah, there you are.'"[25]

African greetings can be long. It is not unusual to engage in an extended line of questions about the condition of your home, children, wife, goats, farm, garden, and work. Greetings can go on for several minutes.

Western cultures view it as a waste of time to spend five minutes saying hello. In a relational culture, there is genuine interest in the other person as an individual. Relationships are important in an African culture. So greetings take a while. It just isn't polite to launch into a conversation without an appropriate greeting.

I was recently in South Africa where they still have gas station attendants who pump gas. An American's tendency would be to roll down the window and say, "Fill it up." In that culture, that would be rude. Good people skills in South Africa include *sawubona* and a few other pleasantries before requesting a full tank.

Sawubona is indicative of a gracious people skill. Some cultures value productivity and time schedules. Villagers in Gadaka where I grew up on the edge of the Sahara desert were more concerned about relationships. No one owned a watch. There were no time sheets to fill in or clocks to punch. Projects could be done tomorrow. As a result, people skills were taught very early in life. Children honored their elders and spoke with respect using appropriate titles. There were specific ways to address all age groups, positions, and stature in society. Greetings were prolonged.

In this village, it was obvious that not everyone had the same level of people skills. Some were coarse. Others were smooth. Some knew how to relate to others exceptionally well. Others remained aloof and recluse. Even in a gracious culture there were those who knew how to connect with others and those who didn't do so well. Those with good people skills became natural leaders.

Interpersonal skills are simply the ability to interact with other people well. It is the aptitude to bring a comfort level immediately to a relationship. It is the skill of putting a damper on the tension in the room. It is the capacity to be liked by the majority of people. It is the ability to relieve pressure in a situation. It is the knack of easily making friends.

Here are some Bible quotes that speak about the topic of people skills:

A soft answer turns away wrath, but a harsh word stirs up anger (Proverbs 15:1).

. . . with all humility and gentleness, with patience, bearing with one another in love, eager to maintain the unity of the Spirit in the bond of peace (Ephesians 4:2-3).

Let no corrupting talk come out of your mouths, but only such as is good for building up, as fits the occasion, that it may give grace to those who hear (Ephesians 4:29).

Be kind to one another, tenderhearted, forgiving one another, as God in Christ forgave you (Ephesians 4:32).

Put on then, as God's chosen ones, holy and beloved, compassionate hearts, kindness, humility, meekness, and patience, bearing with one another and, if one has a complaint against another, forgiving each other; as the Lord has forgiven you, so you also must forgive (Colossians 3:12-13).

You shall not take vengeance or bear a grudge against the sons of your own people, but you shall love your neighbor as yourself: I am the LORD (Leviticus 19:18).

If possible, so far as it depends on you, live peaceably with all (Romans 12:18).

These verses paint the picture of the kind of person you most likely want to be with. These are just nice people. We like people with these characteristics. We feel comfortable around them. Notice some of the key words that flow from these verses:

- Gentleness
- Humility
- Patience
- Peace
- Building up
- Grace
- Kindness
- Tenderhearted
- Meekness
- Forgiving
- Love

These are traits that describe a people person. There is a tendency in Western culture to elevate IQ and knowledge over people skills. Western education applauds the amount of knowledge acquired. Graduation is based on the fact that you passed enough exams. The degree is granted because you read enough books and regurgitated the information.

The irony is that you can finish education with a 4.0 grade point average and fail in a career. Knowledge is indispensable, but it is not the goal. Ultimately, unless a person can relate to others, it is not possible to succeed in leadership. There are some jobs available to people with poor people skills, but they are not leadership roles. Leadership has to do with people, so there must be the ability to connect with others in a meaningful fashion.

This is not complicated.

- Would you rather receive help from an obnoxious person or a gracious person?

- Would you rather spend time with an encourager or a discourager?

- Would you rather be around a pessimist or an optimist?

- Would you like to have dinner with a sarcastic, caustic, and critical person or a gracious, thoughtful individual?

I live in the world of theology and ministry. There are brilliant theologians who lack people skills. They would be happy in a cave lined with books and never interact with people. They understand the academic side of theology and write research papers. They can answer any theological question and debate any issue. They write books. We need these people. They are critical to the strength of the Church. But they cannot lead others because of their hermit-like tendencies.

A person may graduate at the top of his class but fail in the pastorate. Ultimately, a pastor must be able to connect with individuals in the congregation. His role is a shepherd, not a CEO. Some pastors wear out the path between their pulpits and their office without much contact with church members. They may deliver great sermons, but they are not leaders.

Leadership is not just about having the right answer. The delivery system for biblical advice and counseling is through people. If the person with the advice lacks people skills, the answers will not be accepted. There is a familiar statement that is sometimes credited to motivational trainer Zig Ziglar: "They don't care how much you know until they know how much you care."[26]

Here is a little test. Grade yourself on a scale of 1-5.
(1 = weak and 5 = strong)

___ I give my full attention when talking to another person without looking around or letting my thoughts wander.

___ I maintain eye contact 80 percent of the time when talking with someone.

___ I sense that people are immediately comfortable around me.

___ I am considered a kind person.

___ I find people regularly talking to me about personal issues in their life.

___ I am gentle with others.

___ I withhold critical comments until the context is conducive to discretely say something.

___ I regularly frame difficult situations in a positive way.

___ I open up (rather than close) communication channels.

___ I am careful about giving harsh, critical responses.

___ I am a humble person.

___ I am genuinely interested in "them" more than "me."

___ I am more interested in hearing their story than telling mine.

___ I am considered a gracious individual.

___ I find people are drawn to me and want my friendship.

___ I value the opinions of others.

___ I am not defensive.

___ I am self-deprecating.

How did you do? Based on your percentage, what grade do you get? If you are on the low end of the scale, this is great opportunity to improve. If your score is high, there is still room for improvement. None of us are at the top of our game. Everyone can do better.

The question that needs to be answered then is this: How do you learn people skills? There are some who seem to be born with a natural ability to relate to people. Their personality is such that they effortlessly walk into a crowd and take over. They can talk to anyone. But what about the rest of us who were not born with that gene?

A college level course cannot in itself teach people skills. A classroom can identify some facts about people skills, but there is a big chasm between knowing and doing. A skill is the ability to do something. Knowledge is simply having access to the information. So this is not primarily an academic issue.

There are three answers to the question of how to improve our people skills. We develop (1) as we live in obedience to the Word of God and (2) because we are controlled by the Spirit of God, and (3) with the influence of others.

A really good approach for learning a skill is to have a coach. Normally, people skills are based on what we say and how we say it. There are some topics we should not address. There are some topics that need to be addressed—but in the right way. An African proverb from Sierra Leone puts it this way: "Do not tell a man carrying you that he stinks." A person with great people skills could indeed tell someone he stinks and still remain friends.

Those with good people skills can easily coach those who struggle with the "what" and "how." Coaches are invaluable. I am a self-taught golfer and my score regularly demonstrates that. I should have taken golf lessons many years ago. A coach would have immediately corrected some bad habits and established some good patterns in my golf swing. Coaches observe things we cannot see about ourselves.

The same is true of people skills. Someone else can identify what is wrong in your social skills "swing." Go ahead and assume that you do not see yourself as you really are. The Bible says that the heart is deceitful (Jeremiah 17:9). Don't trust yourself in this area. Most of us are oblivious to the idiosyncrasies and extremes of our own personality.

If you push back on that previous sentence, you are proving the statement true. Really. We do not truly understand how others perceive us. None of us can with 100 percent certainty evaluate all our own strengths and weaknesses. That is why we need a people skills coach. We would benefit from having someone watch us in action and evaluate us with objectivity. This needs to be a person who will be straightforward and gracious in his critique—someone from whom you will receive those criticisms without being defensive.

I dare you. Ask a trusted friend to tell you what he thinks about your people skills. You might be surprised. Be assured, he will "see you" as you really are.

Sawubona.

12

PUSHING BOULDERS

The importance of values

I count everything as loss because of the surpassing worth of knowing Christ Jesus my Lord. For his sake I have suffered the loss of all things and count them as rubbish in order that I may gain Christ.
Philippians 3:8

Show me your friend and I will show you your character.
African proverb

lex Haley's book, *Roots*, personalizes the human tragedy of 12 million Africans who were forced into slavery during the 16th to 19th Centuries. His book is the story of Kunta Kinte being captured by contentious tribe members who sold him to slave traders. The slave ship commanded by Captain Davies unloaded him and the other human cargo many months later in Annapolis, Maryland. With a new name, Toby, he began a life as a chattel slave on a southern plantation.

Slave trading of that era is a dark blight on human history. Most would distance themselves from that phase of American history. We had nothing to do with the American Civil War. It is thought to be a thing of the past, yet slavery still takes place today all over the world. Putting other human beings in bondage and treating them as less than human demonstrates the depravity of mankind.

Here is my story of a slight brush with the remnants of the slave trade in West Africa.

For a period of time we lived in a village called Miya. This region had many huge outcroppings of granite. They were massive. Like giant marbles they protruded hundreds of feet out of the ground. Several sides were smooth and un-scalable, but there was normally a way to climb to the top by scrambling up a combination of smaller rocks, trees, and passages.

For a teenage kid, this was great adventure. I spent many hours scaling these peaks and exploring caves and crevices.

The best part was rolling boulders down the mountainside. There always seemed to be a precariously balanced rock that only took a nudge to begin its downward trip. These were often round boulders, four to six feet tall. The results were spectacular. They would start sliding and then roll, picking up momentum, and then bound down the hill with increased velocity. At some point the airborne boulder would crash back onto the side of the mountain and explode, sending fragments like a giant grenade. It was amazing. No fireworks display could be as spectacular.

During one of our boulder-pushing adventures, a villager climbed to the top of the mountain to stop our activities. He was obviously angry. The severity of his reprimand indicated something was seriously wrong.

At the top of some of these mountains were the remains and ruins of villages. The outline of broken-down walls made it obvious that someone had lived on top of these granite outcroppings. It must have been a difficult place to reside. Their farms were below in the flatlands. Water and food was not readily accessible. Getting home meant climbing a mountain.

Why would a civilization live up there? Slavery was the reason for these villages. It was a matter of survival. Living on top meant they had a 360-degree vantage point to watch for slave raiders. Defending themselves was feasible because of their superior position. One of the ways they defended themselves was to have huge boulders strategically positioned to roll down on potential attackers. Those were the stones we were dislodging for entertainment.

The villager's concern was that someday the slave raiders might return, and they would again need to inhabit the mountaintop. That was a crucial issue for this irate villager. For us, boulders were entertainment; for him it was survival. For us, these boulders were playthings; for him it was valuable ammunition.

He was right. We were wrong. We obviously had a different set of values. What was important to him was not important to us.

Values are simply the things that are important to us. We all have them. They show up readily in how we spend our time and money. They are the constant core beliefs, convictions, ideals, assumptions, and standards for which we are most passionate.

Having boulders perched on the side of a mountain was a value to this villager. Not to me. They were merely an opportunity for youthful amusement. But for this descendent of those who had been enslaved, it was of critical importance. He would climb a mountain to stop our fun. He would risk his life dodging boulders to halt our wasteful destruction of this precious resource. For him, this was life-and-death stuff.

That's what values are: things for which we would sacrifice. They are the things for which we really get serious.

You can mess around with a lot of things, but don't mess with my values.

I'm sure this villager had never written a list of core values with *survival* at the top. But staying alive and protecting his family was obviously a value. I didn't have that priority, so boulders were merely a form of amusement. For him, rocks meant life. Values make a major difference in how we act. I had just demonstrated that in a village in Africa.

You can be sure of one thing: you have some core values. You may not be able to articulate them in a list, but you still have them. If someone pushes against your values, you will let them know. They may be spoken or unspoken. They may be written or not. But you can be assured they are there. They may be called the driving force or priorities or guiding principles. Ultimately, they are your most deeply held beliefs.

It gets a little more complex when it comes to team values. Each *member* has a personal set of values and each *team* has its own values. At some point our personal values intersect with others', and that is what forms the group's values. Values exist in corporations, churches, and clubs. Every team has them whether they are articulated or not. You can be sure, however, that there are some things that are important to that group of people.

Few things will break up a team like dissonance in core values. Most group dysfunction comes from failure to agree about values. The team may concur about the mission statement of the group, the vision of the group, or the goals of the group; but if they don't agree on the values, failure is a guaranteed path.

Some have wondered why there are so many churches in town. Other than the doctrinal positions that may differentiate between them, the primary difference is values.

Some churches focus on evangelism. Others are characterized by expository preaching. Still other churches are "family reunion" churches and provide for all generations. There are missions-driven churches, social conscience churches, social justice churches, and classroom churches. Some deem style of music the driving force. In others it is the style of dress or the menu of programs or the formality of the church service. Whatever it is, each church has its distinctives and establishes programs accordingly. Core values are what differentiate between churches.

Differences in values have split more churches than doctrine. Arguments around the board table are most often traced to differences in values. People are normally fired because of a clash of values. Marriages dissolve because of values differences. This is a major issue to be recognized and addressed by any leader.

Core values form the culture of the group. "It is the way we do things around here." Think of the dissimilarities between the KKK, the Girl Scouts, and the Hell's Angels. The thing that makes these organizations so different is the variance in their values. The KKK espouses segregation. Girl

Scouts like cookies and camping. Hell's Angels love leather and motorcycles. These organizations would find it rather difficult to live in harmony. Their values are too different from each other to merge these groups into one.

The organization I lead has the following list of core values:

BIBLICAL TRUTH: A commitment to Scripture as our absolute authority
- We reaffirm bi-annually our convictions expressed in the BMW doctrinal statement.
- We establish churches consistent with the doctrinal position of the mission.
- We apply truth in our relationships.

PRIORITY OF PRAYER: A commitment to our dependence on the power of God
- We believe that God has ordained prayer as a means to accomplish His will.
- We resolve to greatly impact our ministries through intercession.
- We seek to enhance the quality and quantity of prayer within the mission family.
- We desire to promote the quality and quantity of prayer among our constituency.

LOCAL CHURCH: A commitment to working in and through the local church
- We affirm the centrality of the local church.
- We recognize and honor the biblical responsibilities of sending churches.
- We serve sending, supporting, and field churches.

PRIMACY OF RELATIONSHIPS: A commitment to people before programs
- We believe a healthy relationship with God drives our relationships with others.
- We seek to engage in active, daily evangelism through establishing redemptive relationships.
- We value the priority of family relationships.
- We refer to BMW as a family instead of an institution.
- We function as teams, embracing interdependence and accountability.

PURSUIT OF EXCELLENCE: A commitment to quality
- We desire to have everything we do represent Christ well.
- We pursue excellence without excess or extravagance.
- We recognize that excellence is relative to local culture.

SERVANT LEADERSHIP: A commitment to supporting those we lead
- We view servant leadership as an attitudinal reflection of the humility of Christ, while recognizing the importance of organizational structure.
- We are devoted to an attitude of love and service instead of command and control.
- We measure leadership by whether we produce successors; therefore, we are committed to reproducing servant leaders.

LIFE-LONG LEARNING: A commitment to personal and corporate development
- We desire to be life-long learners so that we can be innovative, creative, flexible, and effective without compromising biblical truth.

- We desire a culture that learns from failure and is willing to experiment.
- We actively pursue opportunities for self-improvement, personally and professionally.

Obviously, not every value can be implemented with equal intensity or success. Our organization would never claim perfection. These values articulate direction and points of emphasis. We aspire to these and commit to continual improvement. Putting our core values in writing does a number of things for us.

Recruiting - This immediately lets others know whether they want to join our organization. It is not ethical to be unclear. People don't want to join an organization and discover six months later that their list of values conflicts with co-workers. Listing core values helps to filter people both into and away from the organization. There are many good mission agencies similar to ours, but there are differences that would allow another organization to serve an individual better than if he joined us. We are being transparent and honest to let people know right up front what we elevate to a level of core values.

Decisions - These values assist us in decision-making. There are far too many opportunities out there to tackle all of them. Having a list of core values becomes a grid through which every decision can pass. If the direction being pursued is in conflict with one of our values, the decision has already been made for us. This is not the only decision-making grid we use, but it is one of the most important ones.

Unity - Articulating these values helps to create unity in the organization. There are a couple of consequences if a group cannot agree on their core values: (1) someone will head in a different direction and thus disrupt the team or (2) there will be an inordinate amount of time spent trying to argue about direction. There is far greater potential for harmony if everyone agrees ahead of time about what things are important.

Budgeting - Finances are usually limited, and tough decisions must be made. Those decisions are arbitrary unless there is a set of values to guide the process of crafting the budget. Each line item in a budget should pass the values test. Conversely, you can determine the values of an organization or individual by looking at their budget. Jesus put it this way: *Where your treasure is, there will your heart be also* (Luke 12:34). We spend money on things that are most important to us.

Efficiency - These values help with efficiency and stewardship of time. Once each member of the organization commits to these values, no more time needs to be spent wrestling with them. Time is wasted in a group when there are conflicting values. No matter how inspirational the vision, if there is no unity in values, the group will spend inordinate amounts of time derailed from the main task. The goal is to align mission, vision, and values with strategy. When that happens, the group can then focus on execution rather than on debate.

There does tend to be a hierarchy in values. Some are more important than others. For instance, in our organization, the authority of the Bible is Number One. That is the foundational core value from which everything else flows. That means everything we say, do, or believe cannot conflict with Scripture. For us, that is the starting point. It is the baseline. It is the fountain from which everything else flows. It is the foundation for the rest of the values.

A core values statement is useless if it is hidden in a drawer. This happens regularly with mission statements. It is not uncommon for the leadership of an organization to spend multiple hours crafting a great-sounding purpose statement and then ignore it. The same thing happens with values statements. It is poor stewardship of time to work through a core values list and then hide it away. Here is a little test:

1. Can your leadership team list your core values?

2. Can everyone in your church or organization list your core values?

3. Can you identify specific ways your core values regularly show up in your group?

If you cannot answer in affirmative ways for all three questions, you don't have core values. You have a statement about core values, but you don't have core values. They may be aspirational, but you don't have core values. Your leader may want them to be true, but you don't have core values.

Values are values when they can be identified regularly in the day-to-day life of an organization. They are truly values when an outsider can readily observe them. If values do not show up in behavior, you don't have unity of core values.

So how can the values on the wall show up down the hall? Some possible approaches to making values a reality are:

1. Leaders must model the values.

2. Post the values everywhere possible.

3. Constantly talk about the values.

4. Applaud examples of those who live the values.

5. Make understanding and commitment to the values a prerequisite for joining the organization or being hired.

6. Include values as part of the regular evaluation process.

7. Accept the resignation of those who refuse to hold to the values.

8. Strategize ways to improve implementation of the values.

9. Reward those who demonstrate the values.

10. Periodically do a values inventory.

The big question is whether there is consistency between your stated core values and reality. Does your budget, calendar, and communication match what is most important?

What boulders are so important that you would never push them down the hill?

13

VELD FIRES

The reset button

And he said to them, "Come away by yourselves to a desolate place and rest a while." For many were coming and going, and they had no leisure even to eat.
Mark 6:31

The same sun that melts the wax, hardens the clay.
Nigerien proverb

It is one of my favorite smells. There is nothing like the smoke of an African veld fire. *Veld* is the generic word for the wide-open spaces of Africa. The fields . . . the savannah . . . the quintessential grasslands dotted with umbrella trees. The veld is the skin of Africa.

Much of Africa has two distinct seasons: the dry season and the wet season. When the dry season sets in, it is just that—dry. Totally dry. Not a drop of rain for six months. Everything green turns brown. Dead.

It is near the end of the dry season that veld fires break out. All the grasslands become tinder waiting for ignition. Sometimes lightning starts these fires. Other times they are deliberately or accidentally set by humans. The flames fan across the plain in a wide swath of destruction leaving behind a black path of dirty soot. If the winds are blowing, it turns into a firestorm. Wildlife frantically races to escape. The birds swarm to feast on rodents and small animals that have just lost their canopy of protection.

The smell. That is what I miss the most. The sweet acrid odor of burning grass. In spite of the destruction, there is a beauty to a veld fire.

Veld fires are nature's reset button. There is a destructive side to veld fires. This is part of the natural cycle of life in Africa, and it has positive effects. There are certain seeds that need the heat of a veld fire to start the germination process. The flames dispose of matted dead vegetation and make room for new growth when the rains return. Veld fires are part of the regeneration cycle of plants, trees, and grasses. It is part of the natural fertilization process.

Burned fields are the first to turn green in the spring, even before the first rains. This gives herbivores a head start for the summer grazing. After a winter diet of dry foliage, the green shoots are a welcomed change. Even more importantly, in the spring this nutrition assists the quality of lactation for all the mothers of newborn kudu and zebra.

The Fire Lily is one of the first plants to grow after a veld fire. Two weeks after the embers have died, this scarlet flower blooms, produces its seed, and goes dormant for another ten years. After that another veld fire will awaken the seeds, and out of the ashes comes brilliant beauty.

The Ferncliffe Catchment Conservancy makes the following observation:

> While cattle do not perform well on old, unburned grass, from an ecological point of view it is important to maintain a healthy sward. Not only does this reduce the loss of soil, but also the biodiversity of the area is improved. In experiments in the grasslands of the Drakensberg, it was found that both the small mammals and grass birds, including game birds, benefited from a burn every second year. In the second year after a burn, these animals were found to be most abundant in the grassland, and their numbers started to decline if the grassland was not burned for three years or more. Then there are many of the veld flowers that depend on fire to provide good growing conditions. The rare Hilton daisy is one of these, and two of the best displays of these beautiful flowers can be seen in firebreaks that are burned every year. One of these, at Babanango,

experiences such hot fires that an adjacent wetland has been destroyed by the annual hot fires burning the organic matter, and yet, alongside this destroyed wetland there is a blaze of red flowers every spring.[27]

The veld fire is the reset button of the African savannah. The need to pause and rest is a fundamental principle of life. There is great benefit from coming to a complete stop, taking a breath and then starting up again.

When a computer locks up, we reboot. Electric motors have a reset button when they have been overloaded. It is a safety mechanism to keep them from burning out. We periodically take our car in for a tune up. We recharge our computers, cell phones, and iPads. Measuring instruments like scales are periodically recalibrated. There is no animal, person, or mechanical invention that can run indefinitely without stopping for a rest. Everything needs to reset.

On a Tuesday afternoon of February 2008, Starbucks closed all its stores in the U.S.A. for three hours. Closing 7000 coffee shops for just a few hours meant a loss of $6 million of income. This major corporation understood the importance of hitting the reset button. Their stated purpose was, "We're taking time to perfect our espresso."[28] Coffee is their specialty. It would seem they did not need to improve. Just keep the java flowing. Starbucks took the time to re-train their baristas to assure the perfect cup. They understood the need to press the reset button.

I'm writing this chapter on a cruise. Some would argue that computers should not go on vacation with you, but each of us has a different way to relax. Writing a book is a diversion from my normal work. Some would argue that a missionary should not take vacations, but I do. I always have. Growing up in Africa taught me to value the veld fire.

Taking a break is deeply entrenched in Scripture.

God - God Himself set the ultimate example. After six days of creation He stopped on the seventh day to rest. Since He is omnipotent, He did not need the rest. He could not get tired. It seems the intent of Genesis 2:2 was simply to state that God finished the job of creating. He paused and declared the goodness of all He had done. He set the pace for all who would follow—that there is a time for work and a time to stop working. This is a broad principle that forms the foundation of establishing Sabbaths. This was such a huge issue that God set the example.

Sabbath - God implemented the idea of a sabbath for people. Every seven days, Israel was to stop everything to rest. This was such a high priority that it is one of the Ten Commandments. This was so important that the penalties were severe for those who violated it—severe, as in death penalty. Later, Jesus clarified that the Sabbath was instituted for man, not the other way around. Though the severity of punishment for breaking the Sabbath was lifted, the principle of rest still remains. It was meant to be a gift, not a burden. The human body was not designed to work 365 days a year without taking a break 52 times.

Holy Days - The nation of Israel had seven annual events that were commonly called "feasts." These were times for the people to stop their routine to celebrate or commemorate. These were Passover, Unleavened Bread, First-fruits, Pentecost, Feast of Trumpets, Day of Atonement, and Feast of Tabernacles. The point here is not so much what each of these meant but rather that they were observed. God ordered His people to "reboot" at least seven times a year.

Shemitah - Every seven years was Shemitah for the nation of Israel. Several things happened that year. Debts were forgiven. Fields were left fallow. Farmers stopped planting. Giving the land a break from crops helped to rejuvenate the land.

Jubilee - Every fifty years was the granddaddy of all reset buttons for Israel. This was seven cycles of Shemitah, so on the fiftieth year there was a major break. It was Shemitah on steroids. Slaves were set free. All land was returned to original owners. Everything went back to zero. This was the ultimate of all reset buttons.

The preceding paragraphs indicate a general principle in Scripture. Man is intended to take breaks. It is a principle that we see in the cycle of nature. It is mandatory for both man and machine.

Where I grew up in Africa, there was a tendency to neglect maintenance. The norm was to run a machine until it broke down—then fix it. Vehicles were treated that way. So it wasn't unusual to see buses and lorries parked beside the road with passengers milling around waiting for a part or a mechanic to arrive. Routine maintenance just wasn't part of the culture. The principle of the veld fire never seemed to translate into caring for mechanical things.

One of the safest means of transportation is flying. One of the reasons for this is a tightly regulated maintenance schedule. Neglecting the reset button for an airplane will eventually result in crash and burn. Airplanes make money only when they are in the air. It costs a lot to ground a plane to do upkeep. Even though that is true, there is no airline that would dare neglect maintenance.

In Western culture we do the same thing with our lives. We tend to just keep going until something breaks. Fast-paced, stressful living will eventually break something. Our bodies are not designed to run in the red zone. Like a racecar with the tachometer constantly in the red, our bodies will eventually stop running. It is not possible to constantly have high "revs" without taking a break.

There is a big industry created simply by our neglect of this basic principle. Psychologists, psychiatrists, pharmaceutical companies, doctors, and undertakers make a good living because of neglected reset buttons. Hospitals make a lot of money because people neglect scheduled maintenance of their lives. We can either schedule breaks or be forced to stop when something "breaks."

Churches and organizations also need to stop periodically to assess things. There are basic Christian disciplines from which we never take a break. Things like prayer, Bible reading, evangelism, and worship should never cease. Churches come up with programs as strategies to accomplish certain goals, but these programs are man-made. We should not feel hesitant to stop them once in a while so everyone can take a breather. We came up with the idea, and we should not feel guilty if we stop doing the program. Hitting the reset button on a strategy will enable participants to come back with renewed enthusiasm and commitment.

For both individuals and organizations there needs to be a maintenance schedule. Here are five preset resets for a leader. Get these on your calendar. Make them part of your routine.

Daily (Attitude Adjustment) - Every person needs a quiet time of reflection every day. It is a great way to start the day, even if you are not a morning person. For the Christian, this is a time to read Scripture and pray. Bounding out of bed and straight into the day is a sure path to burnout. Careful meditation on Scripture and spending time in prayer about the day ahead sets the course and the attitude of the day. It is a great time to inventory spiritual, mental, and emotional health.

Weekly (Task Selection) - At the beginning or end of each week it is good strategy to review the past week and build a to-do list for the coming week. This must appear on your calendar and become a habit or you'll live your life by default. The task list is the most practical outcome of the entire process. It itemizes all the practical things to do. This forces you to make deliberate plans for your week. Those plans should flow from annual goals, and your annual goals should flow from your life goals. This assumes, of course, that you have those goals. The basic question to answer is: What do I plan to accomplish this week?

Quarterly (Progress Evaluation) - Ninety days comes around incredibly fast. Unless there are quarterly checkpoints you'll realize on December 31 that the year is already past. Put the following dates in bold on your calendar: January 1, April 1, July 1 and October 1. Unless these dates show up as scheduled maintenance, it won't happen. The quarterly reset is an expanded version of the weekly evaluation. This is a look at a higher elevation. It is a time to review the past quarter and plan for the next ninety days. The basic question to answer is: If I get nothing else done, what are the three things that I need to accomplish in the next three months?

Annually (Goal Setting) - This is much more than making a New Year resolution. It is a time to inventory the previous year and plan for the year ahead. It is a major tune-up, not just an oil change. This is worthy of dedicating an entire day or more to accomplish this task. The broad categories to consider may include health, finances, family, career, spiritual, and social. The basic question to answer is: What do I plan to accomplish this year?

Decade (Vision Casting) - Every five to ten years it is critical to have a major planning event. This is time to refresh the wording of the mission statement. It is time to conduct a major evaluation of the past vision and identify the new one. It requires a major study of present realities that create new challenges and opportunities. This is time to pick the next tree on the horizon for the safari to continue.

Sabbatical (Course Adjustments) - Every 50 years, the nation of Israel observed a year of Jubilee. The frequency meant it would happen only once or twice in a lifetime. This sabbatical is different from the weekly Sabbath. It is longer than a vacation, often several months away from work and routine. The idea is a big break. This is a total overhaul. It is like stripping a car down to the chassis and rebuilding it. There could be several purposes for a sabbatical: furthering education, rejuvenation, re-focusing life, or changing jobs.

Scheduling these six events will not guarantee success, but it is a step in the right direction. These are like a self-imposed veld fire. They will definitely disrupt things for a while, but the results will be worth it.

14

VILLAGE LIFE

Transparency

For if anyone thinks he is something, when he is nothing, he deceives himself.
Galatians 6:3

One falsehood spoils a thousand truths.
African proverb

There is no such thing as privacy in a village of a few hundred people. Everyone knows everything about everyone. No anonymity. A one-room hut means you can't retreat to your own space. There isn't much that happens in town but that everyone knows it immediately. News in the village traveled faster than any digital communication. No such thing as secrets.

Mom never worried about our wandering around the village or out into the bush. She often did not know where we were. That seems rather careless for a mother living in the middle of "deepest, darkest Africa," but everyone knew who I was and where I lived. It was not just my white skin. That was the case with every other kid in the village as well. Everyone knew everyone. Miles away from the village, people would instantly recognize me and could point me back in the right direction.

It also meant that I could not get away with anything. One of the key crops of Northeastern Nigeria was peanuts. The sandy soil, heat, and short growing season seemed to be an excellent combination for growing groundnuts. One of the culinary delights of my youth was to dig up peanuts from the ground and eat them raw. The flavor and texture are completely different and definitely better than dried or roasted.

As a little kid, I loved them. The temptation was to reap them before they were fully developed. Harvesting season could not come soon enough for me. One time the temptation overcame my patience. I went into the farm of a villager and started digging up peanut plants. After the feast, I put the plants back where I found them, expecting that they would continue to grow.

Surely the farmer would not notice a few missing peanuts at harvest time—but he did. There were a couple of things I failed to realize. First, that plants die once they are unearthed. Second, my footprints were easily identifiable from every other kid in the village. There was no dodging the accusation of the farmer. That event became one of frequent opportunities to experience the firm discipline of Dad. At a very young age I learned that there is no such thing as privacy in a village in Africa.

Since we were the only people around with white skin, we were the object of curiosity. The circus had come to town. Everything we did was different, odd, and somehow entertaining to the locals. Dad built a house that was simple yet more Western than a round mud hut. Our house had windows with glass. That meant we literally lived in "a glass house." At any time of the day or night, there could be villagers with noses flattened against the glass, watching us. There was no privacy.

During my teen years, Nigeria experienced a civil war. Southerners had migrated to the North and became wealthy business people. This caused jealousy and then earned the hatred of the Northerners. One morning, without announcement, civil war broke out. The Hausas of the North started killing southern immigrants.

Amazingly, this event was orchestrated and communicated over thousands of miles without radio, telephone, or the Internet. The channels of communication spread like a web to thousands of villages; everyone knew that this was "the" day. The results were horrific. Our first hint of the event was during breakfast as we watched people passing by carrying furniture, beds, and goods that they had ransacked from the homes and businesses of the Ibos from the South. The Biafran War was under way.

I am still amazed at the fact that communication was so prolific, even in a primitive setting. From Africa, I learned the importance of living in community. I observed the value of accountability. It became obvious that there is safety in transparency.

In spite of my upbringing in a village with no walls, I like privacy. Perhaps it is an over-reaction to being village entertainment as a child. American culture, on the other hand, is conducive to doing things in isolation. We value our space. Our wealth enables us to cocoon. Electric garage door openers allow us to unload our cars away from the prying eyes of neighbors. We go places and do things in anonymity. This is so different from other cultures where the whole village knows your business.

I like privacy, but it is dangerous for my wellbeing. Leaders tend to live in glass houses. It is not possible to be a leader without being on exhibit. It is a common complaint of pastors that they are always on display. Leaders work hard at maintaining a private life, but God designed leaders to be out front and on display.

> For you yourselves know how you ought to imitate us, because we were not idle when we were with you, nor did we eat anyone's bread without paying for it, but with toil and labor we worked night and day, that we might not be a burden to any of you. It was not because we do not have that right, but to give you in ourselves an **example** [emphasis added] to imitate (2 Thessalonians 3:7-9).

> Let no one despise you for your youth, but set the believers an **example** [emphasis added] in speech, in conduct, in love, in faith, in purity (1 Timothy 4:12).

> Remember your leaders, those who spoke to you the word of God. Consider the outcome of their way of life, and imitate their faith (Hebrews 13:7).

Leaders need to be visible. It comes with the job. Leading by example is far more powerful than leading by words. If you value privacy, do not become a leader. On the positive side, if you are going to lead, be transparent. People will be watching anyway so why not use it as a leadership tool. Be an example.

One of the common denominators of good leaders is that they are transparent. They tend to be self-deprecating. They do not take themselves seriously. The leader that is not transparent is like the emperor with no clothes. He is the only one out of touch with reality. Followers see the leader for what he really is. If there is any deception, it is self-deception. Since followers often know the real truth about the leader, he might as well admit it openly. He is not hiding anything.

Here is why this is important. A leader out of touch with the reality about himself cannot engender trust. It is appropriately assumed that if you are not aware of yourself, you are probably out of tune with a lot of other things. Since trust is a critical coinage of leadership, transparency is indispensable. Trust is the main currency of effective leaders. Without trust, people will not follow. They want to know you are being forthright with them.

Transparency demonstrates that you will be honest with followers. It shows you are teachable. It shows you are willing to listen, to change, to be honest. When a leader makes himself vulnerable, it makes him accessible, available, and touchable.

The Apostle Paul regularly modeled this principle. He was realistic about himself and let other people know.

> *And I was with you in weakness and in fear and much trembling, and my speech and my message were not in plausible words of wisdom . . .* (1 Corinthians 2:3-4).

> *The saying is trustworthy and deserving of full acceptance, that Christ Jesus came into the world to save sinners, of whom I am the foremost* (1 Timothy 1:15).

For I know that nothing good dwells in me, that is, in my flesh. For I have the desire to do what is right, but not the ability to carry it out. For I do not do the good I want, but the evil I do not want is what I keep on doing. Now if I do what I do not want, it is no longer I who do it, but sin that dwells within me (Romans 7:18-20).

To the weak I became weak, that I might win the weak. I have become all things to all people, that by all means I might save some (1 Corinthians 9:22).

There was a phase when pastors were trained not to be transparent. They were taught never to use themselves as an illustration in their sermons. They did not make friends among the congregation. There was a deliberate strategy to remain aloof and keep a "professional" distance. While this may work for a monarch, it is not good leadership. Alternately, I have noticed that any time I tell a personal story that is less than flattering, someone always shows appreciation for that transparency.

Since few of us live in a small village, we must create our own tribe—a "village" that knows us well . . . a "tribe" with whom we can be transparent . . . a group of people where it is safe to reveal who we really are. Sometimes that happens in a small group in a church. Sometimes it is with close friends. It could happen at work. But for your own wellbeing, it is critical to have a village.

Transparency is not the same as accountability. Secular leadership espouses a top-down model of leadership. That model is designed to "command and control." It is a military motif. It is often summarized in statements like this:

- People do what you inspect rather than what you expect!

- Accountability puts teeth into commitment.

- Accountability forces us to open up for inspection.

These ideas flow from a military or secular work environment. In all those instances, the goal is to get people to do what you want. This is the practical outcome of behavioral psychology but not a biblical model. Scripture teaches us not to pass judgment on others.

> *But with me it is a very small thing that I should be judged by you or by any human court. In fact, I do not even judge myself. For I am not aware of anything against myself, but I am not thereby acquitted. It is the Lord who judges me. Therefore do not pronounce judgment before the time, before the Lord comes, who will bring to light the things now hidden in darkness and will disclose the purposes of the heart. Then each one will receive his commendation from God* (1 Corinthians 4:3-5).

Our accountability is to God. That thought should strike terror in our being. A right view of God will render any need for human accountability useless and redundant. Our transparency is merely living without guile or pretense. Voluntary submission to others gives us an opportunity to practice our accountability to God. It demonstrates a correct understanding of the doctrine of man. It indicates our submission to God and ultimately to each other.

But, what about a verse such as this one?

Obey your leaders and submit to them, for they are keeping watch over your souls, as those who will have to give an account. Let them do this with joy and not with groaning, for that would be of no advantage to you (Hebrews 13:17).

On the surface, this verse might sound like a leader is responsible for the followers' choices. This verse is written, however, to followers, not leaders. It is not teaching leaders to dominate and control others. Just as a teacher might place a copy of her students' report cards in the permanent school records, leaders will someday give a report card to God regarding how well their followers did. That is something quite different from "command and control." The leader's responsibility is to walk in front, not drive from behind. It is a warning that a bad report card is "unprofitable" for the follower.

The primary concern of a good leader is not accountability; it is transparency. I was meeting with a mentor who served as the administrative pastor of one of the wealthiest churches in America. It was said that there were more millionaires per pew in this church than in any other in the country.

My mentor made a statement one day that startled me. He said that the pastor of this church was incredibly insecure. He went on to talk about many other high profile leaders who were dysfunctional because of their insecurities. Eventually, my mentor resigned from his position because it was so difficult to work with this pastor. He was aloof and unapproachable. His lack of transparency morphed into meanness and arrogance.

Leaders need to take the admonition of Paul: *I say to everyone among you not to think of himself more highly than he ought to think* (Romans 12:3). Others may put a leader on a pedestal, but the leader can take himself off. The biblical leader is meant to be an example, and that is hard to do up high and at a distance.

Ultimately, the omniscience of God teaches us that there is no place to hide. If you are struggling with that idea, you might try visiting a small village in Africa. You will get over your privacy issues fast.

15

THE BAOBAB TREE

Rejecting status quo

You have heard that it was said . . . but I say to you . . .
Matthew 5:21-22

*Old carts can be repainted, but they still keep
moving in the same old ruts.*
Mongo Beti, Cameroonian writer

The iconic tree of Africa is the baobab. It is a grossly obese tree with sparse vegetation. The pregnant-looking trunk is massive with spindly branches. It just doesn't look right. Something went wrong with this tree.

African baobab folklore explains that one day God was angry. He pulled up a tree and rammed it back into the earth—but upside down. So the branches that show today are actually the roots; and the roots, now, are on top as branches. This story seems plausible to a villager with an animistic worldview.

The story of the baobab tree illustrates a basic trait of leaders. They look at things differently from most people. Leaders turn things upside down. They think and act differently from most. Like the baobab that seems to be upside down, so too are the ideas and actions of a leader. Leaders think and do what others do not. They often see things the opposite from the crowd.

Jesus' view of things often ran 180 degrees in the opposite direction of popular opinion. Instead of viewing leadership as a hierarchical, top-down organizational structure, He taught bottom-up servant leadership. Instead of earning salvation through works, He taught grace. Instead of condemnation, He offered forgiveness. Instead of retaliation, He told people to turn the other cheek. Instead of hatred, He argued for loving your enemies. He taught that people who were sad, persecuted, poor, and needy were blessed. Almost everything He said and did went against the grain of conventional popular opinion.

That is what leaders do. They swim upstream. They challenge status quo. They see what could be, not just what is. They say and do things that are counterintuitive.

One of the baseline traits of leaders is that they want to change things. They turn trees upside down. This kind of leader does the following:

- Questions commonly held traditions

- Has a respectful suspicion about "the norm"

- Looks for new solutions to old problems

- Feeds an insatiable curiosity

- Carefully assesses the statements and conclusions of others

- Turns assumptions around to examine them from another angle

- Suspends judgment to gather further information

- Longs to make a difference

- Dreams about radical solutions to problems

- Asks not "What is?" but rather "What could be?"

Some people don't really care about the destination. They just want someone else to tell them where the organization is going and they can get it there. We call these people managers. Leaders want to be the ones to decide on the destination. They may not always be so good at getting there, but they know where they want to be. Both managers and leaders are needed in any enterprise. A leader without managers is simply a dreamer. A manager without leaders may just go in circles (though with a good manager the circles will be done well).

There is a fine line between being a leader and a rebel. I serve as the director of a missionary-sending agency that helps churches send missionaries to the field. I have sometimes joked that our recruiting strategy should be to contact all the students who have been kicked out of a Bible college or seminary. I've observed that many of them turn out to be good leaders. They don't fit into the normal student profile. Their expulsion could indicate they are wired to turn baobab trees upside down.

Robert J. Kreigil wrote a book titled *If it Ain't Broke, Break It.* His application was for the business world, but the premise applies to all leadership. Just because everyone else does it "this way" does not mean it is the only way to do it, or even the best way to do it. Inventors, by nature, try to do things others have not tried. At their core, leaders tinker with tradition. They take things that seem to be working well and "break it."

Kreigil writes about NASCAR driver Jeff Gordon who defied conventional wisdom. Most drivers attempt to pass at one specific corner. Gordon practiced passing on the other end of the track because no one expected it there. Defying tradition meant winning more races.

A leader's responsibility is to look down the road to set direction. The new destination on the horizon may take the organization "off road." It means there will be the jolt as the wheels get out of the rut. The ride may be rough. It will cause a lot of questions and discomfort. But that is what leaders do. They create new roads.

Even more disconcerting is that leaders often bring about change when things are going well. They "break it" when it is not broken. They just can't seem to leave well enough alone. Leaders understand that the time to find new paths is when the road is smooth. The temptation is to wait until the bridge washes out, then try to find new direction. But it is much more difficult to do that in the middle of a crisis. Leaders start bringing about change when everything is going well. Followers are tempted to resist because what they are doing is working. The good leader understands the bicycle principle.

Can you imagine riding a bicycle with just one leg? It could work, but it sure would be difficult. Bike riding requires that you press down with your right foot while at the same time bringing your left foot around to then press down with that one. While one leg is doing the work, the next one is getting ready to go to work.

That is how vision casting works. While implementing current goals, the leader must be working on the next ones.

Leading is like riding a bicycle. It requires both pedaling and preparing to pedal. There can never be a time when a leader is not working on BOTH the present vision AND the future vision.

This works on a bicycle but is counterintuitive in other applications. Once there is a plan that is working, the temptation is to leave it alone. But reality is that today's formula will probably not work tomorrow. A good leader will never stop tinkering with the vision.

One of the key performance areas of any leader is to articulate and activate the vision. This *is* the job of leadership. By definition, a leader is a person who is going somewhere and people are following. A leader must know where he is headed and constantly monitor progress. Therefore, a leader should spend time every day either moving the present vision forward or working on the next one. It is a never-ending task.

What commonly occurs is that a leader will clearly articulate a vision for the future but then fail to work on the next one. A set of goals has a lifecycle, and if there is not a new vision to replace the old one, the church or organization will plateau and possibly die. It is counterintuitive for a leader to be thinking about a new vision when he is in the middle of implementing the current plan—but he must!

We have been trained to think that if it ain't broke, don't fix it. The bicycle approach, however, is "If it ain't broke, it will break—someday." Your current plans will not work forever.

You may have tried riding a bike with someone else. One of you pedals while the other person steers. It can work, but ultimately you would never win a race with two on the bike. In the same way, someone must take ownership for creating and guiding the process of identifying the new direction. If the leader doesn't do this, it probably will not get done. Everyone's responsibility becomes no one's job. This is not to imply that the leader creates the vision all by himself. There needs to be a lot of input from others on the team. One person, however, must be responsible to both pedal and steer the bike. We call them leaders.

Getting ready for the next vision is important but not urgent. We are all too familiar with the tyranny of the urgent. As an avalanche of work overwhelms the leader, the tendency is to focus on the avalanche. But leaders must never sacrifice the important on the altar of the urgent. Managing the vision and creating the next one is one of those important things he can do. It is possible to drift without addressing the important, but be assured it cannot be neglected indefinitely.

The one-legged cyclist can get some forward motion, but he would do much better to stop, strap on a prosthesis, and pedal with two legs. The time lost at gaining another leg will very quickly be recouped. Time spent on creating the next vision will ultimately accelerate forward movement.

Therefore the leader must view vision-casting as his job. It is core to his success. It is a major component of his job description.

This means leaders must find time to think. That is, of course, an incredible challenge. The more responsibility a leader has, the less discretionary time he has. It becomes a downward spiral. The faster he goes, the less time he has for creative thinking. The less time he has for creative thinking, the more the downward spiral accelerates. At some point, the leader must step out of the spinning tornado and find a quiet place away from the storm.

There is one thing even more difficult than cycling with one leg: cycling with no legs. If the leader has no vision for the future, there will be no forward movement. The leader must be able to see upside-down trees. He must be able to articulate a preferred future.

Most people ask "Why?" but the baobab-tree-thinking leader asks "Why not?" I love the cartoon of two Eskimos fishing. One is dangling his fishing line through a twelve-inch hole in the ice. The one next to him has carved out a whale-sized hole in the ice that is shaped like a whale. He is thinking differently from most fishermen.

A similar illustration is the well-known story of the two shoe salesmen who went to Africa. The one sent back word to the factory and told them there was no potential for sales. The next salesman wrote back with the message, "Send a shipload—no one has shoes." The leader sees what is possible. He looks at challenges as opportunities. He just thinks differently.

Thinking differently is foundational in the Christian life. Romans 12:2 says, *Do not be conformed to this world, but be transformed by the renewal of your mind.* Non-Christians have one thought pattern. The Bible instructs the Christian to break out of that rut and sees things from a different vantage point. So, in that regard, every Christian leader should have already adopted one of the most fundamental leadership characteristics: turning baobabs upside down.

16

RHINO SKIN

Handling Criticism

For they say, "His letters are weighty and strong,
but his bodily presence is weak,
and his speech of no account."
2 Corinthians 10:10

A leader who does not take advice is not a leader.
Kenyan proverb

R hinos are legendary. They have tough skin that varies between one-half and two inches thick. They are one tough animal and it is not just their skin. There are no natural predators (unless you count humans). None in the animal kingdom challenges this one-ton monster. (As herbivores, their size would argue against eating salad.) No one threatens the rhino. In addition to the buffalo, elephant, leopard, and lion, the rhino is one of "the big five." They earn that name because they are so dangerous to hunt. They fight back.

While they have no natural enemies, they are plagued with pests. Oxpeckers and egrets follow them around riding their backs, picking at their skin. There is some debate about the role of these birds. They do indeed eat the mites and ticks from the hide of the rhino. It is also thought that these birds feed off rhino blood. The blood-engorged ticks are one source of this blood feast. Oxpeckers are also known to keep digging away at a sore, making it worse as they feed on the blood of the rhino.

Every leader has oxpeckers. They hover around leaders. Someone will be a self-appointed critic. There will always be people who peck away with their disapproval. Anyone who has accepted the mantle of leadership has a target painted on his back. It is just part of being a leader.

The Apostle Paul was a spiritual giant, yet he had his critics. *For they say, "His letters are weighty and strong, but his bodily presence is weak, and his speech of no account"* (2 Corinthians 10:10). These were fellow Christians who were on his case. We could understand it if his enemies criticized him, but why would family members go on the attack?

Peter was also the recipient of criticism. He was leading the charge for taking the gospel to Gentiles, but he met resistance. *So when Peter went up to Jerusalem, the circumcision party criticized him, saying, "You went to uncircumcised men and ate with them"* (Acts 11:2-3).

Nehemiah had a goal of rebuilding the walls around Jerusalem. The oxpeckers were there too. This "bird" was called Sanballat.

> *But when Sanballat the Horonite and Tobiah the Ammonite servant and Geshem the Arab heard of it, they jeered at us and despised us and said, "What is this thing that you are doing? Are you rebelling against the king?"* (Nehemiah 2:19).

Everything Nehemiah did was for the good of the nation, but Sanballat became a self-appointed critic.

Moses was one of the most unassuming leaders in history. The Bible calls him meek. He didn't want the job in the first place, but being forced into leadership, he too caught it in the neck.

> *Miriam and Aaron spoke against Moses because of the Cushite woman whom he had married, for he had married a Cushite woman. And they said, "Has the*

LORD indeed spoken only through Moses? Has he not spoken through us also?" (Numbers 12:1-2).

King David was an incredible leader. That did not exempt him from criticism.

When King David came to Bahurim, there came out a man of the family of the house of Saul, whose name was Shimei, the son of Gera, and as he came he cursed continually. And he threw stones at David and at all the servants of King David, and all the people and all the mighty men were on his right hand and on his left. And Shimei said as he cursed, "Get out, get out, you man of blood, you worthless man!" (2 Samuel 16:5-7).

The abundance of evidence shows that leaders will definitely attract criticism. This is not the pleasant side of leadership. No one likes disapproval. It doesn't matter how pure your motives, how diligent your efforts, how careful your decisions, someone will attack. Knowing that you have pure motives makes it that much more difficult to accept unfair judgments. It is difficult to resist fighting back.

Leaders are often in a no-win situation. If they see a potential problem and point out their concern, they are accused of meddling. If the worst happens, they are criticized for not saying something earlier. Either way, someone is going to complain. This is just part of being a leader.

No leader can be perfect, so he normally deserves at least some part of the criticism. But what if you really are flawless? Will there still be criticism? Would anyone dare denigrate a perfect leader? Yes! Jesus was criticized all the time. Even at the height of His greatest act of sacrifice for the human race, people were mocking and jeering while He hung on the cross. In spite of His perfection . . . in spite of His totally pure motives . . . in spite of His sacrifice on their behalf . . . the people ridiculed. If Jesus was the recipient of unfair criticism, we cannot expect any less.

There are, however, a few ways to blunt the sting of criticism.

First, acknowledge that in almost every criticism there is a kernel of truth. It doesn't matter that your enemy has wrong motives for his attack; he has probably identified a weakness in you. While 90 percent of a criticism may be exaggerated or incorrect, there may still be an element of truth. So ultimately, the good leader seeks to learn from the harshest and most unfair criticism. This approach means your enemy has done you a favor. He has helped you to identify an opportunity for improvement.

Second, realize that there will be antagonists because you are doing something. Those who are willing to stand up and get things done make themselves a target. As mentioned earlier in this chapter, Nehemiah knew all about the sting of criticism. He stepped forward and led in a major project of rebuilding the walls of Jerusalem. No one was shooting at him as long as he kept his head down as cupbearer for the king. Once he rose to the challenge of doing something exceptional, he became the target of poisoned-tipped arrows.

The flip side of this principle is that if you are not being criticized, it could be because you are not doing anything worthwhile.

Finally, refuse to retaliate or be defensive. Good leaders can take the hit with a good attitude. Once the leader reacts, he has taken a step backward and loses some leadership capital. Those who hear the criticism know whether or not it is true. Let others come to your defense. It is a person with low self-esteem who lacks the ability to absorb the punch with a smile. Staying in control of self allows the leader to learn from the criticism and demonstrate grace and character to those who follow.

You can either be blessed or blasted by criticism. The choice is yours. The response is under your control. The oxpeckers of your life can be a blessing. They are simply picking away at the imperfect insects of your life. *Whoever heeds instruction is on the path to life, but he who rejects reproof leads others astray* (Proverbs 10:17).

The Australians have an idiom of "cutting down the tall poppies." It is their practice of bringing down anyone who rises above the crowd. As soon as someone stands taller than others because of success, he will be cut down. The message of that culture is to remain average. Leaders cannot succumb to that norm. They must have the tough skin of a rhino and keep charging forward.

It isn't just the Australians who cut down the tall poppies. It happens everywhere. Do something outside of the norm and you will be criticized. Stick your head up above the crowd and it could get chopped off. So criticism may just be a badge of honor. It means you are getting something done.

Brace yourself and welcome the oxpeckers.

17

HEAD LOADS

The art of multitasking

*You shall represent the people before God and bring
their cases to God, and you shall warn them about the
statutes and the laws, and make them know the way in
which they must walk and what they must do.*
Exodus 18:19-20

If you run after two hares, you will catch neither.
African proverb

I t is a classic picture in Africa—the silhouette of a line of ladies walking single file with massive loads balanced on their heads. This is quintessential Africa.

It is a thing of beauty. The grace and balance of an African gliding effortlessly forward with an enormous head-load is one of my favorite memories of the continent. These folk are amazing. Most Westerners do well to keep a hat on their heads, but these people have the incredible ability to walk for miles with huge loads.

I've seen men carry a massive bundle of eight-foot-long firewood. Ladies can balance a four-foot-diameter bundle of thatch or a ten-gallon clay pot full of water on their heads as they return from the well. Anything that can be hoisted, even when it takes two people to get it up there, is carried on the head. It is not uncommon for someone to carry 70 percent of his body weight. Anything can go up top—food, water supplies, fodder, fuel, firewood, hoes, laundry, buckets, basins, tools, or building supplies.

Head loads are an efficient and practical way to carry items for long distances. Even a five-pound weight becomes difficult to carry in your arms for very long. Put it on the head of an African, and he hardly notices that it is there. Good posture eliminates the strain.

That isn't all. African women can carry incredible loads AND at the same time have a baby strapped to her back AND maintain a vibrant conversation AND walk AND weave a basket. All this is done at the same time and with ease. They are the masters of multitasking.

This is a basic trait of good leaders. They must be good at multitasking. But there is a caveat. This does not mean doing many things at the same moment. Researchers are not certain that the brain handles more than one thing at a time. It is probably more like a toggle switch going back and forth rapidly.

The term *continuous partial attention* perhaps more accurately describes what really happens. What the brain can do is shift focus from one thing to the next with astonishing speed. It may seem that the brain can do two things at once, but it is actually moving the switch back and forth quickly.

Teens can look you in the eye, hold a conversation, and at the same time text their friends. The reality is that they are flitting from one activity to another quickly. Even a computer can only do one thing at a time. Because it is so fast, it appears to multitask, but in reality it is jumping back and forth from one task to another.

Thus, multitasking in this context is the ability to move back and forth between several things rapidly. It means the ability to handle multiple projects. Leaders must be able to flip the switch and move effortlessly from one task to the next with calm grace.

Some people prefer to focus on one thing at a time. They like to start one project and work on just that one item until they are finished. Leaders don't have that option. A factory worker on an assembly line can stay focused on putting one nut on one bolt all day long. He doesn't need to think of anything else. A leader cannot operate that way. Leaders must be multitaskers. Some leaders revel in it. They get bored if they have to concentrate on one thing for too long. Some might be accused of having Attention Deficit Disorder, but a leader needs a healthy dose of ADD. Leaders thrive if they can move rapidly from one task to the next.

People who drive while talking on their phones normally drive slower and miss all the details around them. That is what makes their driving dangerous—they cannot concentrate on the details. That may not be good driving, but it is good leading.

Multitasking means a deliberate neglect of details. For a leader, that is okay. The leader needs to focus on the big picture, not the minutiae. Someone else must care for the details so the leader can fly at 30,000 feet.

Here is a sample of the many balls that a typical leader must juggle:

- Lead their "direct reports."
- Advance the current vision.
- Work on the future vision.
- Maintain alignment to the core values.
- Manage multiple projects.
- Build and maintain relationships.
- Promote the organization.

- Motivate and encourage colleagues.
- And then there is the rest of the job description. . . .

Peter Drucker articulates it this way: "Efficiency is doing things right. Effectiveness is doing the right things."[29] The leader must have a frame of reference to know which things to leave undone. Key Performance Areas is one way to accomplish that.

There are three to five things in every job that must be done well in order to succeed. These are the handful of things that any worker with any job must do well in order to succeed. These are the items that can't be delegated.

For instance, a surveyor must be accurate. He might be slow, but he can't be sloppy. If a surveyor wants to keep his job, he has to get it right. The results of inaccuracy mean a building will be built in the wrong place or a road will veer off in the wrong direction.

The idea is to distill all the functions of any job to only three, four, or five key activities. In my job as the director of a nonprofit organization, my key performance areas are as follows:

Board of Directors - No one else in the organization has this role or responsibility. This means I must represent the mission family well to the board and must represent the board well to the mission family.

Direct Reports - There are several men that report directly to me. No one else in the organization will serve them and maintain accountability. This is my role and it cannot be delegated.

Public Relations - There are meetings, functions, activities, and events where I must be present. There is an expectation that only the head of an organization can fill that slot.

Vision - There is no one else in the organization that must focus as much on the over-all direction than the director. Working on the vision appears every day on my to-do list.

Since I am able to list my four major areas of work, it makes it much easier to prioritize my activities and time. This is simple. It cuts through the complexity of a worldwide, nonprofit organization to distill everything to the most important things I must do.

There is no question that a leader must juggle multiple responsibilities; but by identifying his key responsibilities, the leader is able to make the job manageable. The concept of Key Performance Areas provides a context in which to decline other opportunities. Saying no is as important as saying yes. It is a delicate balance between multitasking and overloading.

Since it is not really possible to multitask in the pure sense of the word, a leader needs a system to bring order to potential chaos. He must develop a mechanism for tracking everything that he needs to do. There is one simple strategy to do this: WRITE IT DOWN (or digitize it). Don't trust your memory. May I say it again? Don't trust your memory.

Most of us find it impossible to keep the complexity of leadership in our heads. That means a good leader will have a central location where everything gets recorded. If it is written down, it exists. If not, it doesn't. There are several key items that must be in writing:

- Mission statement
- Core values
- Vision statement
- Annual job description
- Weekly task list
- Notes from meetings and phone calls

Putting things in writing has several benefits. The obvious advantage is that the leader does not need to trust his memory. Leadership is complex, and in the West it takes place in a complex world. Information overload is a crushing reality. A second benefit is that the leader can stay current. If notes from a conversation are written down, he can pick up the discussion six weeks later. Additionally, the leader will create an atmosphere of peace and calm. It is disconcerting for followers to have a leader who is harried and scrambling. Followers want a leader in control of himself and his job.

There are times, however, when leaders need to stop the multitasking. Since leaders deal with complexity, the tendency is to attempt two things at once and do neither of them well.

One instance is communication. When good leaders hold a conversation, they make you feel that you are the only person in the room. It is disconcerting to talk to a distracted person. You know their mind is elsewhere. It is obvious when they are looking around the room and over your shoulder. You are not their priority. So they do a poor job of communicating with you and at the same time send the message that you are not important to them. The leader loses two times.

In one of the many letters he wrote to his son in the 1740s, Lord Chesterfield offered the following advice: "There is time enough for everything in the course of the day if you do but one thing at once; but there is not time enough in the year if you will do two things at a time."[30]

Chesterfield is correct if he means two things at exactly the same time. The effective leader glides forward with calm and grace like an African lady with her head load.

18

WELLS

Creating margin

For this very reason, make every effort to supplement your faith with virtue . . . and knowledge . . . and self-control . . . and steadfastness . . . and godliness . . . for if these qualities are yours and are increasing, they keep you from being ineffective.
2 Peter 1:5-8

*If you eat all your harvest,
you won't have seed for tomorrow.*
African proverb

The village well was critical for the survival of the tribe. You can live without air conditioning, TV, and cell phones, but you must have water. The village well was more than a practical necessity. It was a social gathering place. It was a focal point of village life. It was the place to trade gossip and gather the latest news.

The well in our village was deep because we lived on the edge of the encroaching Sahara desert. I can't remember how deep—just that it took a lot of rope to get to the bottom.

Fetching water was normally women's work. It was an amazing thing to watch them pulling up the water. The "bucket" was a leather pouch that was designed to fill naturally at the bottom of the well. A barefoot woman would catch the attached rope by entwining it around her heel and foot. With a swift backward motion she would pull up six to eight feet of rope, alternately pulling up two to three feet by hand and then the foot again. The rhythm was smooth and seemingly effortless as great lengths of line were quickly piled behind the lady drawing water to the surface. All this was done with a baby strapped to her back and conversations going on with others around the well.

Wells were dug by hand. A man at the bottom of the pit would excavate then put dirt in a basket that was hoisted to the surface by rope. The top of the hole was surrounded with logs entrenched in the ground around the hole. The ropes carved deep grooves into the logs which were often flush with the surface of the ground.

There was, however, a major problem with this arrangement. There was not much of a protective barrier around the gaping mouth of the well. The picture at the beginning of this chapter is of an upgraded well with a retaining wall—a great improvement over the conventional wells. Without the barrier it was not uncommon for a goat or dog to fall in. A decaying animal at the bottom tends to add an unpleasant flavor to the water. A moonless night meant an unsuspecting person could also misstep and end up injured and wet.

This illustrates a fundamental leadership principle: *Barriers are good.* It is possible to stand one inch from the edge of the wide-open hole and not fall in, but barriers provide some margin for error. That is what barriers do— they provide a buffer.

Margin is a major issue in leadership. Successful leaders put up some self-imposed barriers that keep them away from the edge. There are several important barricades for a leader.

Schedule - Leaders are often harried. Their schedules are overloaded. They work long hours. Their calendars are full. Like a bucket filled to the brim, even a little nudge in the schedule spills water creating a mess. A maximized schedule is potentially catastrophic to good leadership.

One of the key responsibilities of a leader is to think. Knowledge workers are paid to think. Someone in the organization must devote time to evaluate the past, present, and future. That doesn't normally appear on any one's time sheet. A leader with a full schedule of meetings and activities does not have time for creative thinking. Thoughtful analysis is part of the leader's responsibility. It cannot be delegated. He cannot be constantly doing. There must be free time to think.

Another key responsibility of a leader is to serve his direct reports. Conventional wisdom limits the number of people a leader works with to less than six. The role of any leader is to lead those people well. No one else in the organization has that responsibility. This also cannot be delegated. A leader must always be available for those who serve close to him. Their needs cannot be put on a calendar. Emergencies cannot be scheduled. The leader must leave time on his calendar for those he leads.

A leader typically works harder and longer than anyone else in the organization, yet he is not a machine. He must have unscheduled gaps in his schedule to catch his breath . . . to muse . . . to reflect . . . to dream.

Margin means working on projects and assignments ridiculously far ahead of the due date. The pastor who prepares his message on Saturday night leaves no room for emergencies. The leader who prepares ten minutes before a meeting should cancel the meeting out of respect for those who will attend. Time seems to accelerate the closer you get to an event. While the minutes on the clock are consistently sixty seconds, the perception is that each minute shortens as you near a deadline. The leader who consistently works ahead rarely faces a crisis of being unprepared.

It seems that the most common area of neglect for a leader is his spouse and children. Many leaders tend toward being workaholics, and the family suffers as a result. A leaders tends to love hisr job, but that often translates into the greatest love of his life. At least that is the way the wife and kids view it. Many a leader has lost his family because of his devotion to the job. If there is any one place a leader must create buffer it is to have time for his loved ones.

In summary: the effective leader leaves empty slots on his calendar to barricade the well of his schedule.

Workload - Everyone has a limit to the size of bucket he can pull from the well. Some can pull thirty gallons at a time; others have a fifteen-gallon capacity. There is no template that gives an industry standard for how much one person can handle. That means a leader must understand himself and then choose the right-sized bucket. That means he can only manage a workload that he can handle. The wise leader knows the size of his bucket and doesn't take on more. He builds a barrier around his workload.

This is one of the values of reporting to someone else. In my instance it is the board of directors. They provide balance and accountability at the same time. My goals and job description are submitted to them once a year at my annual evaluation. It provides a sense of security and wellbeing to have other men affirming my plans and monitoring my workload. Their accountability assures that I am neither lazy nor over-ambitious.

On average, leaders have bigger buckets than followers. It is questionable whether a person with a small bucket will lead many others. The adage is that if you want something done, you ask someone who is busy. That may be another way of recognizing that leaders are able to get more done than others. The person who insists on a small bucket should probably not be a leader.

Integrity - The core working capital of a leader is his reputation. Competency will not compensate for a lack of character, especially with Christian leaders. The primary qualifications of a pastor (1 Timothy 3) are character issues. The one thing that disqualifies a pastor quicker than anything else is lack of godliness. A doctor, architect, mechanic, or truck driver can still do his job if he lacks character. But a pastor cannot. Obviously, other careers would be better advanced if the person had character, but immorality does not disqualify a surgeon. A truck driver can be a liar and still drive a truck. The architect may have a bad family life but still build buildings; however, a Christian leader must be a person of impeccable character.

Followers must be able to trust their leader. Charisma will carry a leader until his reservoir of trust is depleted. That means a leader must put up some barriers that keep him further from the mouth of the well than the average person. This applies to handling finances, expense reports, relationships with the opposite sex, transparency, honesty, and all appearances of propriety. Others may be able to stand at the lip of the well, but the leader cannot.

Finances - The majority of Americans live paycheck to paycheck and under a cloud of debt. That is not fun. It creates incredible tension to be consistently in debt with little possibility of ever being out of the red. The same applies to any organization or business. Spending beyond one's means is foolishness. The good leader builds some barriers to keep from getting to that point.

Remember that we previously addressed the principle where Jesus said that one of the tests of faithfulness (and thus leadership) is how you handle your finances. *If then you have not been faithful in the unrighteous wealth, who will entrust to you the true riches?* (Luke 16:11). Lack of financial responsibility is a disqualifier for leadership. This applies to both nonprofit and for-profit organizations.

This means that a leader must build some financial hedges, both in his personal finances and in the organization he leads. Bankruptcy puts the organization out of business. It is the role of the leader to guard financial solvency. That means having a financial buffer. Spending every penny is like standing with all ten toes over the lip of the well.

Our house was a half mile from the village, so Dad dug a well for our use. His well had a barricade. This was a simple and obvious way to keep a hole in the ground as a place of refreshment without danger. The equally obvious application is for the leader to build some walls around the well of his life and work.

19

THE SWINGING BRIDGE

Succession

*Remember your leaders, those who spoke
the word of God. Consider the outcome of
their way of life, and imitate their faith.*
Hebrews 13:7

*Tomorrow belongs to the people
who prepare for it today.*
African proverb

Our village didn't have a university course on leadership theory. Actually, there were no schools at all. For thousands of years, this village had existed without pen or paper. In spite of that, the people had successfully handed off leadership from one generation to the next. They knew all about succession planning.

These simple village folk were more in touch with their mortality than many in the West. Life was fragile. Death was frequent and often came to the young. They realized there had to be a way to pass on life lessons and leadership skills.

This meant that fathers would teach their sons the life skills of farming and hunting. Mothers would train the girls to cook and care for the family. The elders would meet under the tree in the middle of the village but allow younger men to look over their shoulders and listen in. Passing on leadership was deliberate and continuous. It happened in the natural course of living life. They understood and practiced succession planning.

Because there were no schools in our village, it meant that my sisters and I went off to boarding school. A long drive or a short airplane flight brought us to the campus where we would live and study for nine months of the year. While it was not our first choice to be separated from our parents, this was just the way it was. There were few other options at the time to pursue education in that part of Africa.

One of the routine events during our boarding school days was rest hour. Keep in mind this was Africa. It was hot.

The midday sun was brutal. Not much was stirring, not even the animals. Anyone with any sense got out of the sun and took it easy for a while—except for us kids. We despised rest hour. It seemed to us that this was merely a way to give dorm parents a little bit of a break.

Sunday afternoon rest hour was longer than normal. Thus, when it was finished, there was double the pent-up energy of all these kids. The solution was to take everyone on a Sunday afternoon walk. During the week, we were not allowed off campus. You can imagine trying to manage hundreds of kids if they had freedom to wander the African bush at will. So Sunday walks were a special treat because it took us off campus.

One of our favorite destinations was The Swinging Bridge. It was swinging because of its construction. Cables were anchored on both sides of the gorge with wooden planks forming the deck. Since it was just hanging from cables, the bridge would bounce and sway. It was great fun to get out in the middle and "ride" the bridge.

I remember one day sitting beside a dorm parent after exhausting ourselves with bridge bouncing. We began wondering about the construction of this bridge. The big question was how they got the cables across the gorge in the first place.

Uncle Bill (all adults were addressed as "uncle" or "aunt") told us the story of how they did this. First, someone took a string and climbed down the side of the cliff to the water, swam across, and then climbed up the other side. The string was then used to pull a rope across the expanse. The next rope was thicker in diameter, then a thin cable, and eventually all the thick cables that were the main support for the bridge.

That is a picture of succession. Each generation benefits from the preceding generation. The thin rope of their predecessors enables them to pull a thicker rope across the gorge and eventually build a bridge. None of us are self-made. We all benefit from those who swam rivers and pulled ropes before us.

Jesus made many amazing statements. At the top of the list must be John 14:12. When Jesus was going to leave his disciples, He talked to them about preparing for their future. He said that they and others following would do *greater things*. That is an amazing declaration from someone as extraordinary as Jesus. Who could ever outdo Him? Surely He couldn't be serious.

He was serious. Jesus impacted a few thousand people in His lifetime, but His followers have impacted millions. He rarely traveled outside the borders of His country; His followers have covered the planet. He left a handful of followers, but in one day His disciples saw that number explode to 3000. His fame spread around Israel, but His followers would gain worldwide fame. *Your faith is proclaimed in all the world* (Romans 1:8).

This happened because of the succession-planning strategy of Jesus. Instead of immediately building His empire Himself, He focused on a few, who then built the empire. That is the heart and soul of succession planning. It is the ultimate deferred gratification. It is genuine humility to seek the success of others at the expense of personal fame. Taking the time to train others retards growth. The leader has less to show for his results. But good leaders are more concerned about the success of the next generation than of their own legacy.

This is not an isolated principle. It was in play before Jesus came along. Moses was a mighty deliverer. Though he was an introvert and stuttered, he faced down Pharaoh and liberated his countrymen from this world-dominating politician. He led a million or more people through the obstacles of the Red Sea, of hunger, and of thirst.

In spite of these successes, he didn't get the nation of Israel to their destination. He never fulfilled the vision. It was his protégé, Joshua, who finished the job. It was Joshua who got everyone across the Jordan. It was Joshua who conquered a land and settled everyone in the promised property. Joshua did greater things than his mentor, but he stood on the shoulders of Moses to do it.

Elisha is an illustration of this same principle. His mentor Elijah was an incredible individual. He faced demon worshippers and demonized queens. He spoke with authority and led a nation. All that time, Elisha was shadowing him, watching, learning, absorbing. Elisha's final request from Elijah was a double portion of his spirit, and he got it. In contrast to Elijah's seven recorded miracles, Elisha did eleven. He did greater things.

Another succession story in the Bible is Barnabas and Paul. In the beginning Barnabas was definitely the leader. He initiated the contact with Paul when everyone else was afraid of him. Barnabas brought Paul under his wing and mentored him. Later he would go find him and bring him to Antioch to further his training. The two of them headed off on their first missionary journey together. By the time Paul's second missionary journey began, Barnabas faded into the background and we hear nothing more about him. Paul does *greater things.*

This principle has repeated itself down through history. Succession happens all the time.

- Most of us have never heard of Ghirlandajo. But everyone knows Michelangelo. Ghirlandajo was his mentor. Yet he melted into insignificance, completely overshadowed by his protégé.

- We all know about Beethoven but may not be aware that Franz Joseph Haydn mentored him for three years. We know about Haydn, but we are not sure who mentored him.

- Half of all Nobel prize winners were once apprenticed by other Nobel laureates.

- Every leader I have spoken to about this subject can name one or more people who had a major impact on his success.

HONOR THE PAST

The next generation should always do better than the previous because they have the advantage of learning from those who have gone before. We routinely squeeze ourselves into an airplane with complaints about cattle-car treatment, yet rarely do we stop to think of the Wright brothers who risked their lives on a biplane made of sticks and fabric. They never would have imagined flying 18 hours nonstop at 500 miles per hour. Commercial flying is possible today because the airline industry stands on the shoulders of the Wright brothers.

Pioneers are rarely appreciated during their lifetime. The truth is that without their sacrifice and primitive attempts, we could not do what we do today. The first responsibility in succession planning is to honor those who have gone before us. Like those of us who were bouncing on the swinging bridge, there is little appreciation for the one who took the risk of climbing the cliffs and swimming the river to get the first string across the chasm.

The world record for human pyramids is nine stories tall. You may have seen them. Normally there is a small kid who caps off the top. With arms raised in triumph it seems he is oblivious to the aching shoulders below him that carried all the weight. We dishonor the past by assuming we got here by our own effort.

One of the reasons for honoring the past is that it causes the present generation to do better. There is seriousness about work today because there is a realization of a legacy. When we realize that someone paid an enormous price to get us where we are today, it extinguishes a cavalier attitude and pride. One of the reasons an heir squanders the inheritance is because he didn't work for it.

One of the keys to succession planning is first to honor the past. We are merely one link in a long chain. We don't want to be the missing link between the past and the future.

ADVANCE THE PRESENT

My background is in world missionary endeavor. Succession planning is at the core of this entire enterprise. The one distinguishing mark of mission ministry is that the missionary plans to leave. Success is measured by whether or not a missionary can work himself out of a job.

A pastor, college professor, camp director, or any other kind of Christian minister normally plans to stay indefinitely. A shepherd would like to spend the rest of his life caring for the flock, but it is different in missions. A good missionary has an exit strategy before he ever gets started on a project. So in my world we are forced to mentor the next generation. Yet every endeavor, business, nonprofit organization, or church would benefit from having a succession mindset. This is not just for missionaries.

INVEST FOR THE FUTURE

Primitive cultures tend to be more concerned about the next generation than technologically advanced cultures. The Patriarchs of the Old Testament were deeply concerned about blessing the next several generations. They embodied the adage that there is no success without a successor. There are two ways to do that. First, find a mentor. Second, be a mentor.

If you have never had one, find one. It is rather arrogant to think you don't need to improve in some area of your life. We all need input. We all have blind spots. A good mentor will point out areas of improvement and fuel the fires of forward movement. To have a mentor will mean that you need to approach that individual and ask for his time. Rarely will someone decline. He will feel honored you have asked. Be sure to clearly state what you want and how much time you are asking for. Let him know what you are asking of him and how frequently you want to meet. Assure him that you will come with the questions and he doesn't need to prepare. You are just asking for his time and input from his experience. Be specific.

Jack Welch was the CEO of GE, the largest company in the world. He put it this way: "Before you are a leader, success is all about growing yourself. When you become a leader, success is all about growing others."[31] Succession planning results in both the mentor and the protégé becoming better leaders. Mentees ask great questions and sharpen the thinking of a mentor. It causes them to reevaluate what they are doing and how they do it. It normally results in followers going further and faster. It often means the organization or business does far better than if mentoring did not exist.

To be a mentor to someone demonstrates a view for the future. It acknowledges the value of others and puts their success ahead of yours. It makes both you and your protégé better leaders.

The Bridge Builder
By Will Allen Dromgoole

An old man, going a lone highway,
Came, at the evening, cold and gray,
To a chasm, vast, and deep, and wide,
Through which was flowing a sullen tide.
The old man crossed in the twilight dim;
The sullen stream had no fears for him;
But he turned, when safe on the other side,
And built a bridge to span the tide.

"Old man," said a fellow pilgrim, near,
"You are wasting strength with building here;
Your journey will end with the ending day;
You never again must pass this way;
You have crossed the chasm, deep and wide—
Why build you a bridge at the eventide?"

The builder lifted his old gray head:
"Good friend, in the path I have come," he said,
"There followeth after me today,
A youth, whose feet must pass this way.
This chasm, that has been naught to me,
To that fair-haired youth may a pitfall be.
He, too, must cross in the twilight dim;
Good friend, I am building the bridge for him."[32]

20

GOING ROGUE

The danger of success and getting old

*I have fought the good fight, I have finished the race,
I have kept the faith.*
2 Timothy 4:7

Because he lost his reputation, he lost a kingdom.
Ethiopian proverb

African elephants are the largest land animal on earth. They are majestic. At 12,000 pounds and ten feet tall, they can intimidate anyone and anything. Elephants don't worry much about predators.

The norm is to live in herds within a matriarchal social structure. The largest female leads the group of eight to one hundred elephants in a tight family unit. At the age of twelve to fifteen years the males leave the group and begin a new family. There is always a dominant male in the herd, but sooner or later, a younger male will take over, and the older ones are left to wander alone. It is a melancholy scene to watch a great-grandfather pachyderm grazing completely by himself.

For whatever reason, some of these older males go berserk; they go rogue. Unstable males become violent and territorial. They go on a rampage, attacking anyone in their way, destroying crops and vegetation. These are the really scary guys.

Unstable elephant males become violent and territorial. That describes some human leaders as well. We might immediately think of Adolf Hitler or Idi Amin. They are well known, but there are thousands of other leaders who have acted the same way. They just didn't have as big a platform on which to act out their rampage.

The irony is that rogues often get that way after some success. These are not normally young leaders. They are often at the stage of life where they have reached a level of success. They have built an empire, and their territorial nature leads them to think they own the place. They are difficult to work for. They may even become violent—at least in words.

Nothing is as dangerous as success. Few leaders can handle it. Something can be triggered inside when a leader has a positive track record. Going rogue results in a god-complex and leaders start acting it out. They are the boss. They bark commands and demand compliance. Their word is law. They must not be questioned. They have established their kingdom, and all serfs must bow in reverence. They are unstable males who have become violent and territorial.

There seems to be a fork in the road as leaders age. It often happens in their 60s or 70s. They either become gracious or caustic. One road leads to a mellowing; the other leads to harshness. The path a leader takes is a choice, but it is not just one choice. It is a lifetime of choices that culminate in an accelerated downhill race to the finish. Tendencies of a lifetime become accentuated and exaggerated. Idiosyncrasies that are managed and suppressed in younger years may become unleashed in later life.

Like the old rogue elephant, a rogue leader may end up wandering the savannah of life as a loner, kicked out of the herd. He may still be kicking up the dust and trumpeting, but everyone around him wants him out of the group.

There comes a time in every leadership role when the individual becomes a liability. He may have been a productive part of the herd, but there is a point at which he is no longer an asset. There is a time when his group participation ceases to be productive.

The trick is knowing when to step away before the herd kicks you out. Leaving the leadership role before things sour is an art form. There is no scientific formula for making a decision. Since I have not yet experienced this, I find it difficult to write on this topic. Perhaps this chapter should be another book a decade or two from now, but I have observed the rogue scenario enough to know I don't want to be one.

Christian leaders often brag that they will die with their boots on and that there is no such thing as retirement in the Bible. But the reality is that most cannot keep their physical stamina and mental acuity right up to the end, especially if they live a long life. They may want to die with their boots on, but normally it is a good idea to take them off when they are in a hospital bed. There is no dishonor in stepping away from a leadership role before you must.

African leaders are renowned for staying too long. Their aspiration is president for life. The common saying on the continent is, "One man, one vote, one time." Nelson Mandela was the exception. He stepped away for the presidency of South Africa long before he needed to. He was still mentally and physically doing very well, yet he was determined to set an example to the rest of the African leaders that they should not aspire to life-long positions.

Going rogue is not an isolated situation in the leadership world. The Bible is full of examples.

Moses successfully pulled off a major coup and ransomed a million people from bondage, performed multiple miracles, and personally talked with God. Yet he blew it late in life and failed to cross the Jordan and finish his task. Moses went rogue.

David penned poetry that resonates with people to this day and was considered a man after God's own heart. Yet late in life he betrayed his marriage vows and then murdered Bathsheba's husband. David went rogue.

Solomon was the smartest guy in the room . . . any room . . . any time . . . anywhere. Yet at the end of his life he turned against the very God who had granted all his wisdom and wealth. Solomon went rogue.

Uzziah reigned over Israel for fifty-two incredibly successful years. He was one of the most productive, godly, and famous kings. He won wars and fueled the economy of the nation to prosperity. Yet toward the end of his life he became proud and he self-destructed. Uzziah went rogue.

Noah pulled off one of the greatest feats of faith in human history and earned a place in the Hebrews hall of faith. Yet after all his success we find him in a drunken stupor. Noah went rogue.

Lot walked away from the decadence and debauchery of one of the most corrupt cultures of his day, yet he ended his life in a drunken, incestuous relationship with his daughters. Lot went rogue.

Judas was one of The Twelve, one of the chosen few. This elite corps of men lived with Jesus, the creator God. He witnessed the miracles, went on mission trips, and was held in high esteem for his proximity to Christ. Yet those "successes" did not keep him from a notorious ending. Judas went rogue.

Demas was a co-worker with the famous Apostle Paul. He was part of the winning church-planting team. He saw the power of God in people's lives and the success of a massive church-planting initiative. Demas went rogue.

I play golf. I didn't say I am a golfer. I just play golf. The older I get, it seems I do better on the front nine than the back nine. Perhaps it is lack of stamina and focus. It is just getting harder to finish the last hole with the same concentration and strength as I had on the first hole. This may be a microcosm of life. It seems counterintuitive that failure would come later in life, yet the stories from the Bible that are listed in this chapter are all about men who failed during the "back nine." I've noticed repeatedly that, in the ministry, more men fail later in life than earlier in life.

It is really difficult to finish well. One of the few leaders in the Bible to do so was the Apostle Paul. He was able to pen the following last words before the executioner arrived at his prison cell: *The time of my departure has come. I have fought the good fight, I have finished the race, I have kept the faith* (2 Timothy 4:6-7). Paul was exceptional. The tendency for leaders is to go rogue.

I'm not there yet (I don't think), but I am concerned about this next phase of my life. In preparation I've been thinking about this subject and asking a lot of questions. So the following is merely theory. I haven't put it to the test, but here is my strategy to keep from going rogue.

1. Be aware that this is possible. Merely the fact that this is on my radar must surely have some value. It is not going to catch me by surprise. I realize I have the potential of going rogue. Just knowing that fact must surely be a good step in the right direction.

2. Guard my daily walk. It seems that leaders who go rogue did not just wake up one day a different person. It was a lifetime of habits and patterns that became accelerated and accentuated with age. I'm assuming the bad parts of me will only be worse with age. Now is the time to monitor my actions and attitudes. What I sow today will come to fruition later on.

3. Ask for accountability. I have asked three people who know me well and see me regularly to let me know if they see I'm "losing it." I've watched boards agonize over letting the CEO go because he no longer "has it." It is awkward to tell someone that he is going rogue. Therefore, I have invited three people to approach me without any fear of reprisal. They know I'll be greatly disappointed if they see me going rogue and don't tell me.

"Unstable males become violent and territorial." That accurately describes rogue elephants. I hope it never describes me.

APPENDIX A

How can church leaders know whether a man is ready to begin pastoring? What attributes, abilities, and experiences should he have before being ordained for ministry?" The list below, created by church-planting missionaries in South Africa, incorporates not only the biblical character mandates, but the knowledge, skills, and basic experiences a person should have to be ordained to minister as an elder, pastor, or missionary.

Review the list. In the second column, write a number from 1 (least) to 5 (best) of your preparedness in that area.

OUTCOME OBJECTIVES Attributes, Abilities, and Experiences FAMILY	1-5
• His marriage, family, work, and personal life are God-pleasing, consistent, integrated, and balanced.	
• He is a godly leader of his wife and children.	
• His wife has some level of formal education and has received personal mentoring.	
• His wife is supportive of him training in the church-based program and of his future ministry.	
• Their children, if still at home, live an orderly life, not given to open rebellion or immoral conduct.	
• He and his wife are both hospitable and share what God has provided for them.	
• He and his wife understand the public nature of pastoral ministry, guidelines for alleviating the pressures it can have on a pastor's family, etc.	

• He is family-oriented in his affections and scheduling and not given to overworking.	
• Finances. He can live on a budget, pays bills on time, and is not in debt (except for appreciable items such as a house).	

CHARACTER

• He has a high and biblical view of God, Christ, and the Scripture.	
• He is oriented to Scripture-based priorities, planning, and problem resolution.	
• He understands his personality, strengths, giftedness, weaknesses, and tendencies.	
• He has a serious and appropriate view of self and is committed to life-long learning.	
• He has a love of people and can balance the demands of tasks and people.	
• He evidences the manifestation of the fruit and gifts of one filled with the Word and the Holy Spirit.	
• He has an eager desire to serve as a leader (deacon, elder, or pastor).	
• He is blameless and above reproach; he has a "Teflon life" (no accusation hurled at him will stick).	
• He has a good reputation with people in the marketplace, at work, at school, etc.	
• He is temperate and self-controlled.	
• He is generally self-disciplined in his habits of eating, driving, TV viewing, sports/hobbies, budgeting, etc.	
• Although he may have a sense of humor, he is generally a serious person and thinks honestly about himself and others close to him.	
• He has good behavior and will apologize when he has engaged in wrong or questionable conduct.	
• He must be honest and be a man of his word; he mustn't promise too hastily or be double-tongued.	

• He is not given to wine or other addictive substances.	
• He is not violent in speech, gestures, or actions.	
• He is not greedy for money and does not gamble or partake in schemes to get money without working suitably for it.	
• He responds biblically when corrected and looks for truth in any criticism.	
• He responds biblically when offended/ wronged.	
• He invites periodic, positive criticism of his ministry by his leadership.	
• He responds appropriately to changes in circumstances.	
• He is a team player when set among other leaders and is not quarrelsome or autocratic.	
• He understands that ministry is "people work" and has good people skills.	
• He has a meek and gentle spirit.	
• He understands that leadership means serving others.	
• He finishes tasks undertaken correctly and on time unless properly delegated.	
• He can keep a confidence.	
• He has a daily devotional life and is committed to regular study of God's Word.	
• He diligently keeps a clear conscience before the Lord and others and is quick to confess, repent, and forsake a known sin.	
• He does not covet positions and is not overly ambitious.	
• He understands and has demonstrated the value of time management, punctuality, and scheduling.	
• He keeps a personal book containing a daily log of activities, appointments, schedules, calendars, addresses, and phone numbers, etc.	
• He manages his time well.	

• He understands the principles of biblical decision-making.	
• He has established and updated short-, medium-, and long-term goals and understands strategic planning.	
• He has an understanding of priorities and conflicting interests and can say no to good things.	
CHURCH-RELATED SKILLS	
PASTORING	
• He is fully prepared for ordination.	
• He is committed to having a deep prayer life.	
• He has a good grasp of shepherding— leading, feeding, comforting, and protecting the flock.	
• He knows how to provide meaningful comfort and practical help to those who are grieving.	
• He understands the different leadership styles, giftedness, and temperament types of people that he ministers with and to.	
• He has thought through and developed a written philosophy of ministry.	
• He has demonstrated the ability to interact and work well with other church leaders on various levels.	
• He is familiar with biblical and popular methods of church growth and their strengths and weaknesses.	
• He is familiar with church structure concepts such as cell or growth groups, discipleship networks, etc.	
• He has a biblical position on major social issues.	
• He knows how to apply Scripture practically to the situations of life.	
PULPIT MINISTRY	
• He is committed to regular study of the Word and has sound exegetical skills.	

• He can communicate effectively God's truth either one-on-one or to a group.	
• He can present the Word in both topical and expository formats and knows the pros and cons of both.	
• He knows the methods and guidelines for conducting weddings and funerals and infant dedications.	
• He has experience in conducting the Lord's Table and baptisms.	
EVANGELISM	
• He evangelizes along the way and actively builds relationships with unbelievers.	
• He is familiar with different evangelistic styles, i.e., testimonial, confrontational, etc.	
• He can make smooth transitions to spiritual topics.	
• He is familiar with evangelism training courses.	
• He is familiar with various evangelism methods such as street, puppet, and musical evangelism, etc.	
• He is familiar with the needs of the culture or community in which he evangelizes.	
COUNSELING	
• He is familiar with the principles of biblical counseling, confidentiality, accountability, etc.	
• He is generally familiar with popular but unbiblical philosophies and psychologies and can explain the differences.	
• He knows how to apply Scripture practically to the situations of life in counseling.	
• He understands the value of, and guidelines for, in-home visits of visitors and church families.	
• He understands the value of, and guidelines for, visiting the sick.	

• He understands the value of, and guidelines for, encouragement of families of the sick or deceased.	
DEACON & ELDER	
• He meets the biblical qualifications for an elder or deacon.	
• He has learned mediation and conflict-resolution skills.	
• He is able to confront graciously and in a supportive, pro-active manner.	
• He is familiar with the pros and cons of various models of church governance and has a preferred model supported by the Scripture.	
• He is thoroughly acquainted with the guidelines and procedures involved in church discipline of leaders and church members and its possible repercussions.	
• He can recognize men suitable for church leadership and can recognize unqualified persons.	
DISCIPLESHIP	
• He understands the importance of having a discipleship ministry with other young men, and he can and has discipled other believers.	
• He fully understands the concept of church-based leadership development.	
• He understands the importance of training men who give families and the church stability and leadership.	
• He is familiar with biblical passages on discipleship and the different models of discipleship.	
ADMINISTRATION	
• He can administer a church's ministries and office.	
• He is willing to delegate to those who may not do the job as well as he can.	
• He understands the balance between keeping a schedule and keeping flexible.	

• He understands basic organizational accounting.	
• He can organize and manage personnel, volunteers, and paid staff.	
• He knows who and where his administrative and service resources are.	
• He understands that the Constitution and By-Laws are a limitation on the exercise of arbitrary authority, and that they bind him to certain requirements and procedures in the running of the church.	
MISSIONS	
• He understands the global responsibilities of his local church in reproducing church-planting churches here and abroad.	
• He understands how regular and periodic missions giving fits into a church's budget.	
• He is thoroughly acquainted with the church planting process and the various models of church planting.	
• He understands the virtues of a good missions program and policy and the characteristics of a poor one.	
ADULT EDUCATION	
• He is familiar with general teaching methods, course preparation, text selection, lesson plans, class decorum, and teaching skills.	
• He is familiar with the differences between preaching and teaching and knows how to adjust his teaching to the level of his students.	
• He has designed and taught a church-based education course.	
USHERING	
• He can schedule and administer an ushering/greeting staff.	
• He is familiar with the use and storage of various forms of church literature such as bulletins, brochures, visitors' cards, tracts, display tables, sign-up sheets, etc.	

• He has experience in greeting, seating, and taking offerings.	
• He understands the importance of first impressions of visitors, and the vital role of the usher.	
MUSIC MINISTRY	
• He can lead singing and choose music for a church service.	
• He knows biblical principles concerning music, what is unbiblical, what is preference, and how to deal with other music issues using scriptural doctrine for this dispensation.	
SUNDAY SCHOOL	
• He can design a Sunday School curriculum plan for pre-school through high school age groups.	
• He can design a series of lessons with lesson plans appropriate to each age group.	
• He can capably use media in teaching.	
• He has a basic knowledge of available Sunday School curricula.	
• He can train and assist others in developing lesson plans.	
YOUTH MINISTRIES	
• He is able to design and implement a youth program for Grades 1 through 12.	
• He is familiar with resources for youth programs.	
• He is familiar with guidelines for running a youth program, both as to education and activities.	
LADIES MINISTRY	
• He can teach an appropriate ladies' study, course, or Sunday School.	
• He is familiar with the differences and dangers of working with and counseling women.	
• His wife (if he is married) is able to capably lead a ladies' Bible study.	
NURSERY	

• He can organize a nursery ministry.	
• He can capably and creatively work in a nursery.	
• He can schedule and motivate nursery personnel.	
• He can order and oversee supplies for nursery such as snacks, drinks, diapers, toys, fans, heaters, etc.	
INTERPERSONAL SKILLS *(see also Character, above)*	
• He is conversant and shows a genuine interest in people.	
• He demonstrates the skill of encouragement.	
• He mixes and interacts well with people.	
• He is aware of his people- or task-orientation and is able to keep a proper balance between the two.	
• He is aware of cultural differences between people groups due to class, race, ethnicity, background, location, national history, etc., and he adapts well to differing classes and cultures.	
• He has a slightly higher than societal average ability to use the language in which he ministers.	
• He is not overly opinionated, is careful about stating opinion as fact, is not threatened by opposing opinions and does not make excessive reference to self in conversations.	
COGNITIVE SKILLS	
• He can think critically and analytically.	
• He can follow detailed reasoning fairly well.	
• He knows why he believes what he believes and can support his views with Scripture.	
• He knows the differences between conviction and preference and between what is biblical and what is cultural.	

• He desires to be a life-long student and has demonstrated the habit of personal study.	
• He can recognize trends in society and predict consequences.	
• He knows where and who his academic and theological resources are for research and self-improvement.	

COMMUNICATION SKILLS *(see also Pulpit Ministry above)*

• He clearly communicates ideas in writing.	
• He has a good working knowledge of grammar, vocabulary, and punctuation.	
• He understands that different contexts demand differing use of writing styles.	
• He has good reading comprehension and speed.	

BIBLE & THEOLOGICAL KNOWLEDGE

• The Scripture is the final authority in his life and teaching and ministry.	
• He has a good working knowledge of the Scripture.	
• He is familiar with the themes, major divisions, authors, dates, and contexts of every book of the Bible and can explain how each gives us a picture of Christ.	
• He can explain the significance of key New and Old Testament passages.	
• He has memorized at least 200 verses of Scripture.	
• He has taught at least 3 Old Testament books and 3 New Testament books to adult audiences.	
• He is able to exegete and interpret the Scriptures literally, grammatically, and historically for use in sermons, teaching, and discipleship.	
• He has prepared and given at least 50 different sermons.	
• He has a working knowledge of Theology (Systematic, Biblical and Historical).	

• He is familiar with the span of Church History and the major heresies and reformation movements.	
• He is familiar with the religions, cults, and "isms" of the last two centuries and can detect and refute false teaching, error, and wrong doctrine.	
• He is familiar with the alphabet and basic nouns and verbs of Greek and Hebrew and knows how to use original language tools. Even with these, he must confess that he is under-equipped to use the original languages effectively and accurately.	
• He is very familiar with and has used research tools such as commentaries, Bible and theological dictionaries, interlinear texts, lexicons, etc.	
• He operates with an understanding of the different levels of dogmatism; i.e., the difference between speculation, opinion, supported belief, and convictions.	

PERSONAL SKILLS

• He has a language aptitude for any foreign language in which he hopes to minister.	
• He is computer literate, with good abilities in word processing and desktop publishing.	
• He understands the principles of professional dress.	

PRACTICAL MINISTRY TOOLS

• If technologically and financially feasible, he uses appropriate and current technology for communication.	
• He has access to at least one good set of conservative commentaries.	
• He has study tools such as concordances, an inter-linear text, Bible dictionaries, and theological dictionaries.	
• He has at least five different English versions of the Bible.	

• He has at least three books dealing with the history of the church.	
• He has a systematic theology text.	
• He has at least three apologetics books.	
• He has at least ten books on marriage, the family, raising of children, etc.	

OUTCOME OBJECTIVES FOR A LEADING LADY

Titus 2 makes it clear that women are to train women. But what does a fully trained lady look like? What is the profile of a woman who is fully equipped to impact the lives of others? The following is an inventory to help develop some goals for training.

Review the list. In the second column, write a number from 1 (least) to 5 (best) of your preparedness in that area.

OUTCOME OBJECTIVES	1-5
Attributes, Abilities, and Experiences	
FAMILY	
• Her marriage is God-pleasing, consistent, integrated, and balanced.	
• Her family is God-pleasing, consistent, integrated and balanced.	
• Her work is God-pleasing, consistent, integrated, and balanced.	
• Her personal life is God-pleasing, consistent, integrated, and balanced.	
• She influences other toward godliness.	
• She has received personal mentoring.	
• Her children, if still at home, live an orderly life, not given to open rebellion or immoral conduct.	
• She is hospitable and shares what God has provided.	
• She understands the public nature of pastoral ministry, guidelines for alleviating the pressures it can have on a pastor's family, etc.	
• She is family-oriented in her affections and scheduling and not given to overworking.	
• Finances. She can live on a budget, pays bills on time, and is not in debt (except for appreciable items such as a house).	
• She pays attention to personal grooming and modesty.	

CHARACTER

• She has a high and biblical view of God, Christ, and the Scripture.	
• She is oriented to Scripture-based priorities.	
• She understands her personality, strengths, and giftedness.	
• She understands her personality, weaknesses, and tendencies.	
• She has a serious and appropriate view of self and is committed to life-long learning.	
• She has a love of people and can balance the demands of tasks and people.	
• She evidences the manifestation of the fruit and gifts of one filled with the Word and the Holy Spirit.	
• She has a willing desire to serve as a leader.	
• She is blameless and above reproach; she has a "Teflon life" (no accusation hurled at her will stick).	
• She has a good reputation with people in the marketplace, at work, at school, etc.	
• She is temperate and self-controlled.	
• She is generally self-disciplined in her habits of eating, driving, TV viewing, sports/hobbies, budgeting, etc.	
• Although she may have a sense of humor, she is generally a serious person and thinks honestly about herself and others close to her.	
• She has good behavior and will apologize when she has engaged in wrong or questionable conduct.	
• She is honest and a person of her word; doesn't promise too hastily or is double-tongued.	
• She is not controlled by alcohol or other addictive substances.	
• She is not violent in speech, gestures, or actions.	

• She is not greedy for money or partakes in schemes to get money without working suitably for it.	
• She responds biblically when corrected and looks for truth in any criticism.	
• She responds appropriately to changes in circumstances.	
• She is faithful in "little things."	
• She responds biblically when offended/wronged.	
• She invites periodic positive criticism of her ministry.	
• She is a team player when set among other leaders and is not quarrelsome or autocratic.	
• She understands that ministry is "people work" and has good people skills.	
• She has a meek and gentle spirit.	
• She understands that leadership means serving others.	
• She finishes tasks undertaken correctly and on time unless properly delegated.	
• She can keep a confidence.	
• She has a daily devotional life and is committed to regular study of God's Word.	
• She diligently keeps a clear conscience before the Lord and others and is quick to confess, repent, and forsake a known sin.	
• She does not covet positions and is not overly ambitious.	
• She understands and has demonstrated the value of time management, punctuality, and scheduling.	
• She keeps a personal book containing a daily log of activities, appointments, schedules, calendars, addresses, and phone numbers, etc.	
• She manages her time well.	
• She understands the principles of biblical decision-making.	

• She has established and updated short-, medium-, and long-term goals and understands strategic planning.	
• She has an understanding of priorities and conflicting interests and can say no to good things.	

CHURCH-RELATED SKILLS

MENTORING	
• She has discipled a new believer.	
• She is committed to having a deep prayer life.	
• She has a good grasp of concepts of mentoring.	
• She knows how to provide meaningful comfort and practical help to those who are grieving.	
• She understands the different leadership styles, giftedness, and temperament types of people that she ministers with and to.	
• She has thought through and developed a written philosophy of ministry.	
• She has demonstrated the ability to interact and work well with other leaders on various levels.	
• She has the people skills to relate to different kinds of people.	
• She is familiar with church structure concepts such as cell or growth groups, discipleship networks, etc.	
• She understands the balance of focusing on a few while ministering to many.	
• She has a biblical position on major social issues.	
• She knows how to apply Scripture practically to the situations of life.	

TEACHING MINISTRY	
• She is committed to regular study of the Word.	
• She has sound exegetical skills.	

• She can effectively communicate God's truth either one-on-one or to a group.	
• She can present the Word in a systematic way so that people understand the text.	
• She can conduct a ladies' Bible study.	
• She can facilitate a Bible study discussion group.	
EVANGELISM	
• She evangelizes along the way and actively builds relationships with unbelievers.	
• She is familiar with different evangelistic styles, i.e., testimonial, confrontational, etc.	
• She can make smooth transitions to spiritual topics.	
• She has led another person to Christ.	
• She is familiar with various stages of evangelism.	
• She is familiar with the needs of the culture or community in which she evangelizes.	
COUNSELING	
• She is familiar with the principles of biblical counseling, confidentiality, accountability, etc.	
• She is generally familiar with popular but unbiblical philosophies and psychologies.	
• She knows how to apply Scripture practically to the situations of life in counseling.	
• She understands the value of, and guidelines for, in-home visits of visitors and church families.	
• She understands the value of, and guidelines for, visiting the sick.	
• She understands the value of, and guidelines for, encouragement of families of the sick or deceased.	
LEADERSHIP	
• She meets the biblical qualifications of a Titus 2 woman.	
• She has learned mediation and conflict-resolution skills.	

• She is able to confront graciously and in a supportive, pro-active manner.	
• She understands the principles of servant leadership	
• She has a high level of ambiguity tolerance.	
• She has a plan of life-long learning and self-improvement.	
• She can recognize others who have potential for leadership.	
DISCIPLESHIP	
• She understands the importance of having a discipleship ministry with other young ladies.	
• She fully understands the concept of church-based leadership development.	
• She understands the importance of training women who give families and the church stability.	
• She is familiar with biblical passages on discipleship and the different models of discipleship.	
ADMINISTRATION	
• She can organize special events.	
• She is willing to delegate to those who may not do the job as well as she can.	
• She understands the balance between keeping a schedule and keeping flexible.	
• She can organize and manage personnel, volunteers, and paid staff.	
• She knows who and where her administrative and service resources are.	
• She knows how to manage a household.	
• She knows how to manage a project and keep within budget.	
• She has secretarial skills (i.e. church calendars, newsletters, etc.)	
MISSIONS	
• She understands the global responsibilities of her local church in reproducing church-planting churches here and abroad.	

• She understands the virtues of a good missions program and policy, and the characteristics of a poor one.	
• She has gone on a missions trip.	
• She knows how to practically and creatively minister to missionaries.	
• She understands how regular and periodic missions giving fits into a church's budget.	
• She is thoroughly acquainted with the church planting process and the various models of church planting.	
• She demonstrates a heart for the missionary and her mission field.	
• She is able to pass on information to the church that keeps people informed of the missionary's needs.	
• She can effectively help develop and organize a missions conference.	
ADULT EDUCATION	
• She is familiar with general teaching methods, course preparation, text selection, lesson plans, class decorum, and teaching skills.	
• She knows how to adjust her teaching to the level of her students.	
• She has designed and taught an adult education course.	
HOSPITALITY	
• She has a desire to deepen her relationship with people through hospitality.	
• She has the cooking skills to provide attractive meals for visitors.	
• She understands the importance of first impressions of visitors, and the vital role of making visitors welcome to her home or church meetings.	
SUNDAY SCHOOL	
• She can design a series of lessons with lesson plans appropriate to each age group.	
• She can capably use media in teaching.	

• She has a basic knowledge of available Sunday School curricula.	
• She can train and assist others in developing lesson plans and learning to teach.	
• She is capable of maintaining discipline in a classroom.	
• She understands characteristics of different age groups.	
LADIES MINISTRY	
• She can teach an appropriate ladies' study, course, or Sunday School.	
• She is familiar with the differences and dangers of working with and counseling men.	
• She is able to capably lead a ladies' Bible study.	
NURSERY	
• She can organize a nursery ministry.	
• She can capably and creatively work in a nursery.	
• She can schedule and motivate nursery personnel.	
• She can order and oversee supplies for nursery such as snacks, drinks, diapers, toys, fans, heaters, etc.	
INTERPERSONAL SKILLS *(see also Character, above)*	
• She is conversant and shows a genuine interest in people.	
• She demonstrates the skill of encouragement.	
• She mixes and interacts well with people.	
• She is aware of her people- or task-orientation, and is able to keep a proper balance between the two.	
• She is not overly opinionated and is careful about stating opinion as fact.	
• She is not threatened by opposing opinions.	
• She does not make excessive reference to self in conversations.	

• She is aware of cultural differences between people groups due to class, race, ethnicity, background, location, national history, etc., and she adapts well to different cultures.	
• She has a slightly higher than societal average ability to use the language in which she works.	

COGNITIVE SKILLS

• She can think critically and analytically.	
• She can follow detailed reasoning fairly well.	
• She knows why she believes what she believes and can support her views with Scripture.	
• She knows the differences between conviction and preference and between what is biblical and what is cultural.	
• She desires to be a life-long student and has demonstrated the habit of personal study.	
• She can recognize trends in society and predict consequences.	
• She knows where and who her academic and theological resources are for research and self-improvement.	

COMMUNICATION SKILLS

• She clearly communicates ideas in writing.	
• She has a good working knowledge of grammar, vocabulary, and punctuation.	
• She understands that different contexts demand differing use of writing styles.	
• She has good reading comprehension and speed.	

BIBLE & THEOLOGICAL KNOWLEDGE

• The Scripture is the final authority in her life and teaching and ministry.	
• She has attended classroom learning sessions.	
• She has a good working knowledge of the Scripture.	

• She is familiar with the themes, major divisions, authors, dates, and contexts of every book of the Bible and can explain how each gives us a picture of Christ.	
• She can explain the significance of key New and Old Testament passages.	
• She has memorized at least 200 verses of Scripture.	
• She is able to exegete and interpret the Scriptures literally, grammatically, and historically for use in teaching and discipleship.	
• She has prepared and given at least 50 different lessons.	
• She has a working knowledge of Theology (Systematic, Biblical, and Historical).	
• She is familiar with the religions, cults, and "isms" of the last two centuries and can detect and refute false teaching, error, and wrong doctrine.	
• She is very familiar with and has used research tools such as commentaries, Bible and theological dictionaries, interlinear texts, lexicons, etc.	
PERSONAL SKILLS	
• She has a language aptitude for any foreign language in which she hopes to minister.	
• She is computer literate, with good abilities in word processing and desktop publishing.	
• She understands the principles of professional dress.	
PRACTICAL MINISTRY TOOLS	
• If technologically and financially feasible, she uses appropriate and current technology for communication.	
• She has access to at least one good set of conservative commentaries.	
• She has at least five different English versions of the Bible.	
• She has a systematic theology text.	

• She has at least ten books on marriage, the family, raising of children, etc.	
• She has a least one book on apologetics.	

APPENDIX B

A CHURCH LEADER CAN LEAD BY . . .

PERSONAL INFLUENCE

Relationships	The congregation thinks or knows that:
We know and love him well, he knows and loves us well, and we trust each other.	_____ You are friends with them and with those to whom you minister. _____ You spend time with families outside of regular church activities. _____ You know how people in the congregation think and react. _____ You sincerely seek out the opinions of others on issues and ideas. _____ You have a good sense of humor and can laugh at yourself. _____ You have a shepherd's heart. _____ You are approachable and non-threatening. _____ You are known well enough for people to trust your judgment. _____ You are more concerned about individuals than the organization.

Earned Respect	The congregation thinks or knows that:
We don't know him well, but he is a fine man of God who has repeatedly shown us that he has the skills of wise and godly leadership.	_____ Your proposals for change are biblically based and well thought out. _____ You are a life-long learner and keep reading to keep learning. _____ You are a person of integrity and enthusiasm, and you motivate change. _____ You have been in the church for years, and you know the community and culture. _____ You seem to be interested in the congregation, not in your personal success. _____ You are not threatened by those with greater ability or different opinions. _____ You encourage benign dissent. _____ You listen to the congregation and are patient enough to build consensus. _____ You seem to have a good walk with the Lord. _____ You have the ability to counsel and to handle crises. _____ You have the ability to administrate and organize.
Accorded Respect *We don't know him well, but he seems nice and we'll listen to his ideas.*	The congregation thinks or knows that: _____ You have ties to church families and the community. _____ You have expertise in this area of ministry. _____ You have general experience in ministry. _____ You have an earned or honorary doctorate. _____ You have a seminary degree. _____ You have a Bible or Christian college degree.

ORGANIZATIONAL AUTHORITY	
The Power of Position *We follow him because he's a boss. Hopefully he knows what he's doing.*	The congregation thinks or knows that: _____The organizational documents permit leaders to make changes at their discretion. _____The culture of the church dictates that leaders make the decisions. _____The lay church leaders are low functioning and agree with whatever is proposed. _____You use personal charisma and bold speeches to overcome resistance.

CORRUPT INFLUENCE	
Maneuvering & Manipulation *We can't dialogue without being suspect, and those who challenge him are soon in big trouble. He's going to do what he wants.*	The congregation thinks or knows that: _____You confuse your program with scriptural principles, so that opposing you is viewed as opposing God's Word. _____You don't mention the downside of any changes that will take place. _____You discourage independent thinking. _____You suppress opposing ideas by intimidation or not allowing them on the agenda. _____You engage in political maneuvering by turning others against those who question or oppose you. _____You use threats or manipulation to get your plans adopted. _____You force people who oppose you off of committees or boards. _____You control the employment of staff so that they fear to express concern or dissent.

APPENDIX C
EVALUATING MY LEADERSHIP
Rate yourself (1= low, 5 = high)

Medicine man	I lead primarily through influence.	
Lions	I am in a consistent and measureable learning mode for leadership.	
Lorries	I understand and implement paradigm shifts.	
Mai Haji	I am constantly working on the vision of the group I lead.	
Anthills	I am exceptional in my teamwork skills.	
Dodo	I consistently define reality in my leadership style.	
First Rain	I manage time well—both *chronos* and *kairos*.	
Hornbills	I am characterized by servant leadership.	
Mud Hut	I am characterized by making the complex simple.	
Blacksmith	I am regularly coaching and mentoring others for leadership.	
Sawubona	I excel in my people skills.	
Boulders	I live out a clear set of core values.	
Veld Fires	I have a set of reset buttons built into my life and work.	
Village Life	I live a transparent life of integrity.	
Baobab	I am constantly dissatisfied with the status quo.	
Rhino	I value and learn from criticism.	
Head Loads	I do well at handling multiple projects.	
Wells	I have margin built into the critical areas of my life.	
Swinging Bridge	I am actively involved in developing my successors.	
Going Rogue	I am definitely on a track to finish well.	

NOTES

[1] n.d. http://quotegeek.com/literature/antoine-de-saint-exupery/3015/ (accessed May 7, 2013).

[2] Blanchard, Kenneth. *Lead Like Jesus.* Thomas Nelson, 2005.

[3] n.d. http://www.priestsforlife.org/mother-teresa/breakfast-letter.htm (accessed May 7, 2013).

[4] Robertson, C., ed. *Dictionary of Quotations.* 1998.

[5] MacGregor, Roy. *Wayne Gretzky's Ghost: And Other Tales from a Lifetime in Hockey.* Vintage Canada, 2012.

[6] Calaprice, Alice, ed. *New Quotable Einstein.* n.d.

[7] Thorpe, Scott. *How to Think Like Einstein.* Sourcebooks, 2000.

[8] Swindoll, Charles. *Growing Strong in the Seasons of Life.* Zondervan, 1994.

[9] Niven, Paul R. *Balanced Scorecard Step-by-Step: Maximizing Performance and Maintaining Results.* John Wiley & Sons, 2006.

[10] Smith, Hyrum W. *10 Natural Laws of Successful Time and Life Management.* Warner Books, 1994.

[11] Blanchard, Ken, and Steve Gottry. *The On-Time, On-Target Manager: How a "Last-Minute Manager" Conquered Procrastination.* New York, Harper Collins Publishers, 2004.

[12] Depree, Max. *Leadership Is an Art.* Doubleday, 1990.

[13] Temkin, Bruce. *The Six Laws of Customer Experience*. Temkin Group, 2012.

[14] n.d. http://www.digitaltrends.com/features/top-10-bad-tech-predictions/3/ (accessed May 7, 2013).

[15] Ibid.

[16] n.d. http://www.memorable-quotes.com/ken+olsen,a1725.html (accessed May 7, 2013).

[17] n.d. http://www.digitaltrends.com/features/top-10-bad-tech-predictions/3/ (accessed May 7, 2013).

[18] MacArthur, John. *The Master's Plan for the Church*. Chicago: The Moody Bible Institute, 1991.

[19] Edwards, Gene. *A Tale of Three Kings*. Tyndale House Publishers, 1980.

[20] Collins, Jim. *Good to Great*. Harper, 2001.

[21] n.d. http://www.cloverquotes.com/quote/by/albert-einstein/23628-simplicity-understand (accessed May 7, 2013).

[22] Fulkerson, Norman. *An American Knight: The Life of Colonel John W. Ripley, USMC*. The American Society for the Defense of Tradition, Family and Property, 2009.

[23] Vautier, John M., and John J. Vautier. *Speak As Well As You Think - An Executive's Guide to Excellence in Public Speaking*. Nostina, 2013.

[24] Lavoie, Richard. *The Motivation Breakthrough: 6 Secrets to Turning On the Tuned-Out Child*. Simon & Schuster, 2007.

25 Claxton, Guy, and Bill Lucas. *Be Creative: Essential Steps to Revitalize Your Work and Life*. BBC Books, 2004.

26 Hogan, Kevin. *The Science of Influence: How to Get Anyone to Say "Yes" in 8 Minutes or Less!* John Wiley & Sons, 2011.

27 n.d. http://www.ferncliffeconservancy.co.za/article5/ (accessed May 7, 2013).

28 Schultz, Howard, and Joanne Gordon. *Onward: How Starbucks Fought for Its Life Without Losing Its Soul*. Rodale Books, 2011.

29 Drucker, Peter, and Peter Ferdinand Drucke. *Management: Tasks, Responsibilities, Practices*. Butterworth-Heinemann, 1999.

30 Chang, Larry, ed. *Wisdom for the Soul: Five Millennia of Prescriptions for Spiritual Healing*. Gnosophia Publishers, 2006.

31 Lowe, Janet. *Jack Welch Speaks: Wit and Wisdom from the World's Greatest Business Leader*. John Wiley & Sons, 2008.

32 Felleman, Hazel, and Edward Frank Allen. *Best Loved Poems of the American People*. Doubleday, 1936.

Made in the USA
Middletown, DE
11 June 2022

66956834R00149